Death by Regulation

Death by Regulation

How Bureaucrats Killed One of Obamacare's Promising Innovations

PETER L. BEILENSON, MD, MPH

Johns Hopkins University Press
Baltimore

Johns Hopkins University Press
2715 North Charles Street
Baltimore, Maryland 21218-4363
www.press.jhu.edu

Library of Congress Cataloging-in-Publication Data

Names: Beilenson, Peter L., author.
Title: Death by regulation : how bureaucrats killed one of Obamacare's
    promising innovations / Peter L. Beilenson, MD, MPH.
Description: Baltimore : Johns Hopkins University Press, 2019. | Includes
    index.
Identifiers: LCCN 2018057303 | ISBN 9781421432144 (pbk. : alk. paper) |
    ISBN 9781421432151 (electronic) | ISBN 1421432145 (pbk. : alk. paper) |
    ISBN 1421432153 (electronic)
Subjects: | MESH: United States. Patient Protection and Affordable Care Act.
    | Delivery of Health Care—organization & administration | Delivery of
    Health Care—legislation & jurisprudence | Politics | Health Care
    Reform—history | Insurance, Health—legislation & jurisprudence | United
    States
Classification: LCC RA412.2 | NLM W 84 AA1 | DDC 368.38/200973—dc23
LC record available at https://lccn.loc.gov/2018057303

A catalog record for this book is available from the British Library.

*Special discounts are available for bulk purchases of this book. For more
information, please contact Special Sales at 410-516-6936 or specialsales@press
.jhu.edu.*

To my parents,
Tony and Dolores Beilenson,
for their lifelong love and advice

and

To my wife and best friend,
Chris, for her love, devotion,
and stalwart support

and

To my children,
Valerie, Alex, Jane, Jack, and Hank,
and my grandson, Noah, for just being
themselves

Contents

Death by Regulation

Prologue

As a child growing up in California during the 1960s and 1970s, a new form of healthcare was available to my family—the health maintenance organization (HMO); in our case, Kaiser Permanente. In theory, HMOs were incentivized to provide preventive care as well as sick care because they paid providers in advance each month (a practice called capitation) to care for their panel of patients, and providers and the HMO were rewarded for keeping their members healthy. Thus, the interests of patient, provider, and insurance company were aligned. In Kaiser's case, this is a fair representation of how the system actually worked.

Patients tended to stay with Kaiser for considerably longer than with traditional insurers, so it paid (literally) for Kaiser physicians to offer preventive service and education, because the injury or illness they prevented would have been on Kaiser's dime. I remember being counseled by my Kaiser pediatrician, Dr. Clifford Skinner, about wearing a bike helmet at age 9—decades before helmets were required—and, at age 12, about the dangers of smoking. Both messages were the right thing to say ethically and factually, but they also could prevent unnecessary expenditures by Kaiser for head injuries or respiratory conditions.

The only negative part of the Kaiser experience was that the care was provided in a large, depersonalized center. Though I liked my doctor and nurse practitioner, I remember to this day that I found the facility was particularly forbidding and unwelcoming.

Havana, Cuba, 1999

In the spring of 1999, my seventh year as Baltimore City health commissioner, my wife, Chris, and I led a delegation of health officials to Cuba. As an official delegation—recognized by both the American and Cuban governments—we obtained a fascinating view of the remarkable system of healthcare there.

Hampered by the American embargo on virtually all medical materiel and relying on diminishing quantities of Russian supplies, Cuban hospital care was negatively affected. Though the physicians were generally quite good, the lack of supplies often led to substandard care.

On the other hand, the Cuban system of primary care was both effective and well-liked by patients. A physician and nurse team from neighborhood-based health centers delivered primary care. Responsible for the health outcomes of their neighborhood, the doctor and nurse team was motivated to deliver preventive services to keep from sending their patients to regional specialists or to the regional hospital. Thus, home visits were made to shutins, and special efforts were made to get every child immunized, by going to their homes if need be. From our visits to several typical primary care offices, it was obvious that the doctor and nurse knew their patients well. The offices emanated a sense of family. This system of preventive and primary care is the main reason that, by many indices (from immunization rates to life expectancy), Cuban health outcomes equal or surpass those of the United States.

Howard County, Maryland, 2007

In 2007, about the time Barack Obama announced his candidacy for president, Ken Ulman, the county executive of Howard County, Maryland, appointed me health director of the county. Howard is the wealthiest county in the wealthiest state in the country—a suburban jurisdiction halfway between Baltimore and Washington, DC—and it didn't have many of the public health problems endemic in those two urban areas. Having served previously as the health commissioner for nearby Baltimore City for thirteen years, I approached the new job with mixed emotions: trepidation over whether there would be issues interesting enough to sink my teeth into as there had been in Baltimore, and excitement over the passion Ulman had for pursuing an innovative health policy for his county.

Indeed, that is about how my five years in Howard County played out: not having to spend much time on public health problems facing more challenged jurisdictions—lead poisoning, sexually transmitted infections, gun violence, post-traumatic stress disorder in schools—but being able to launch innovative initiatives, such as recognizing healthy schools, workplaces, and restaurants by setting standards that, if followed, gained accreditation for these institutions as a Healthy Howard site. This led to increased usage of these sites by health-conscious Howard Countians.

Our most innovative and ambitious initiative, however, was to create a quasi-insurance plan for the uninsured of Howard County—which became known as the Healthy Howard Access Plan. As a wealthy county, Howard had a significantly smaller percentage of uninsured residents than the majority of counties in Maryland or the United States. However, the 2007 Census Bureau statistics showed that 8% of the county's residents did not have health insurance, which meant that about 20,000 individuals were uninsured. After setting aside those above 300% of the federal poverty level (an income of about $70,000 for a family of four, at that time), under the assumption that they could afford at least meager insurance on their own, and those below 116% of the federal poverty level—who were eligible for, but not yet enrolled in Medicaid (federal/state health insurance covering the poor)—the universe of uninsured Howard County residents eligible for our plan was in the range of 8,000 to 12,000 individuals.

Because we wanted to make it as easy as possible for uninsured residents to gain coverage, regardless of income, we created the "Door to Health Care." Uninsured Howard residents simply had to come—in person or virtually—to the "Door," where staff would obtain basic information about income and family size. Those who were eligible for Medicaid were assisted in applying for that program, while those whose incomes were too high for Medicaid were assisted in enrolling in Healthy Howard.

Those who enrolled in Healthy Howard paid a nominal "premium" of $50 to \$75 per month for individuals and \$85 to \$115 per month for a couple. In return, they received up to seven primary care visits a year with our primary care partner—Chase Brexton Health Services, whose primary care center was conveniently located in the middle of the county. We worked with a wide range of specialists and were able to enlist providers in almost every major specialty to provide pro bono care to our Healthy Howard members, and Howard County General Hospital (owned by Johns Hopkins Medicine) agreed not to bill any of our members for their hospital stay. We also worked with our providers to prescribe less expensive generic medications and with pharmaceutical companies' pharmacy assistance programs to obtain some brand medications for free for our members. To bolster these services, we hired health coaches, who would meet face-to-face with our members to develop personalized health and wellness plans. This innovative coaching program was eventually found by Johns Hopkins researchers to significantly change our members' attitudes and behaviors and won an award from the US Department of Health and Human Services as one of the ten most innovative health programs in the country.

We announced that the initial open enrollment period for Healthy Howard would take place at the East Columbia Public Library on October 10, 2008. Not sure how many to expect, we were pleasantly surprised to see lines going out the door. By the end of the first two days, over 1,100 Howard County residents had applied to Healthy Howard. As it turned out, only 66 were eligible for the program—and they were quickly enrolled. However, several hundred were eligible for the much more robust Medicaid program and were enrolled in it. Thus, within the first month of the launch of the Healthy Howard program, more than 1,000 residents obtained health coverage they had not had before.

Over time, approximately 2,000 Howard County residents joined the Healthy Howard plan, and thousands more were enrolled in Medicaid through the Door to Health Care, resulting in an impressive drop in the number of uninsured county residents. Indeed, the percentage of the uninsured decreased to levels that would be reached in other jurisdictions only with the implementation of the Patient Protection and Affordable Care Act several years later.

Despite the general success of Healthy Howard, it was simply not a replicable model for the State of Maryland, or even for Howard County in the long run. Clearly, we could not expect hospitals and specialists around the state to cover all of the 750,000 uninsured Marylanders for free. Rather, we saw Healthy Howard as a bridge to a broader form of healthcare reform that was soon to be promoted by the newly elected president, Barack Obama.

Prologue as the Future

What do these three disparate locales with stories from three different decades have to do with one another? The structure of Evergreen Health Cooperative and our affiliated primary care offices were a direct outgrowth of my experiences—both personal and professional—with these three different but complementary healthcare systems.

PART I / A CO-OP Is Launched

Chapter One

Creating Evergreen

March 2010 to March 2013

After lengthy negotiations and intensely partisan debates over a two-year period early in the Obama administration, the Patient Protection and Affordable Care Act (ACA) passed the US Congress. On March 23, 2010, it was signed into law by the president. From there began the massive undertaking of developing the innumerable rules and regulations that would be necessary to implement the many initiatives of the far-reaching act. One such initiative enabled the formation of nonprofit health insurance cooperatives (CO-OPs) in each state.

Created as a sop to liberals after the "public option" section of the bill (a government-run alternative to private insurance) was lost in the legislative process, the CO-OPs were mostly an afterthought. Pushed by powerful senators from farm states, particularly Kent Conrad (D-ND) and Max Baucus (D-MT), where cooperatives were popular (albeit not health insurance cooperatives), the CO-OP program emerged as section 1322 of the ACA, when the smoke cleared from the final battles over the legislation.

The CO-OPs were technically not a typical cooperative, where members owned a portion of the entity, as is the case with some purchasing cooperatives. Instead, they were Consumer Operated and Oriented Plans. The idea was to create new competition in each of the states where CO-OPs would be developed in order to lower health insurance premiums and encourage innovation in those markets.

When the CO-OP program started, it was given almost no chance of success. I later learned from one of the leaders of the nascent CO-OP movement, John Morrison (the former Montana state insurance commissioner), that during the ACA negotiations, a congressional staffer who had helped write the ACA went so far as to say that the CO-OP section of the bill was considered to be a "plastic plant"—it was designed to sit on the window sill and look nice, but no one imagined it would ever grow. Also unbeknownst to us at the time, Barbara Smith, the US Health and Human Services official who was hired to implement the program, was told that HHS would consider the program a success if she got two or three of the entities off the ground. State insurance regulators publicly expressed skepticism that anyone would form a CO-OP, as did health insurance trade publications and think tanks.

However, by the spring of 2011, various groups that were considering forming CO-OPs became acquainted and began weekly telephone calls to exchange information and ideas. A group of entrepreneurs in Montana, led by Morrison, the former Montana insurance commissioner, formed the National Alliance of State Health CO-OPs (NASHCO) to serve as a trade and advocacy organization for the new entities. NASHCO held a conference in Washington, DC, in the summer of 2011, which was attended by nearly 100 people interested in forming or working with CO-OPs.

Throughout 2011, in a series of public meetings of the CO-OP program advisory board, various guidelines were proposed. This process was important because the language in the ACA creating the CO-OPs was quite vague about requirements. This dearth of guidance gave a lot of leeway to the secretary of HHS and, by extension, its subordinate agency responsible for much of the implementation of the ACA, the Centers for Medicare and Medicaid Services (CMS), to develop rules on how the CO-OP program would function.

Discussions at the NASHCO conference revealed a critical chicken-and-egg problem: The application process, which required a feasibility study with actuarial analysis and a proposed business plan and budget, would cost on the order of $100,000, a sum that few of the hopeful CO-OP developers had or could raise.

However, several early CO-OP founders reached out to existing entities like hospitals and physician groups in their home states that were potentially interested in partnering with these foundling CO-OPs—an arrangement that might substantially improve the CO-OPs' chances of success. One of these visionaries was Ken Lalime, who was the head of an independent physicians association (IPA) and would become the CEO of Connecticut's CO-OP. According to Lalime, while attending the 2011 NASHCO conference, he asked himself why his IPA should "work with external payers" when he could "be a payer—[who] already had the network of providers to work with." Indeed, after doing several market assessments, he thought the marketplace was "incredibly in need of a not-for-profit . . . Market research showed a niche and we could make a hit by good customer service and low prices . . . I thought the prognosis was good, looked to grab 10% of small group market out of a handful of payers in first year of operation 2014."

This line of reasoning helped lead to an unexpected profusion of CO-OP applications. By the end of 2012, still many months from the first open enrollment period under the ACA, twenty-three CO-OPs from twenty-two states (Oregon had two) had been approved and given contracts committing a total of $2 billion in capital loans. Moreover, forty-some applications had been completed, submitted to CMS, and were awaiting consideration. Defying all expectations, CO-OPs in nearly all states appeared imminent. The twenty-three successful applicants had officially joined and funded NASHCO, and discussions had begun concerning nationwide group purchasing of services such as actuarial support, insurance product development, and claims paying. Similarly, the concept of network reciprocity, in which CO-OPs would share national networks of contracted physicians and hospitals, was explored. If these agreements came to fruition, there could be significant economies of scale for the participating CO-OPs, lowering their costs substantially and making them more competitive in their markets than a typical new entrant would be. Thus, the prospect of a truly national integrated CO-OP presence in the health insurance market, with all its transformative potential, had suddenly become very real.

Originally, the CO-OP program was to be funded with up to $10 billion of government grants distributed to at least one CO-OP in each of the fifty states. However, the early organizational success of the CO-OPs did not go unnoticed by the existing health insurance industry and its defenders, resulting in the grants becoming loans. Oversight committees in Congress showered the CO-OP applicants with burdensome document requests, including detailed twenty-year budgets, a far longer period than required of any other insurance company. Conservative media outlets issued stories predicting CO-OP failure, and the same lobbyists that killed the public option during the consideration of the ACA quietly went to work with the White House and Congress to terminate the CO-OP threat.

The conclusion of the insurance industry's machinations came literally in the eleventh hour of the so-called fiscal cliff deal, on December 31, 2012. CO-OP developers awakened on New Year's Day 2013 to read that Congress had rescinded all funding for CO-OPs that were not already under contract and prohibited any further loans to CO-OP applicants, including those that were scheduled to sign their final loan documents in the first few days of 2013. CMS's CO-OP program coordinator, Barbara Smith, had no inkling that this radical alteration of the CO-OP program was in the works. The dozens of groups that invested in CO-OP applications that were pending were left holding the bag. As if this cloak and dagger process were not enough, Smith's two-year contract with CMS expired at year's end, and the agency made the decision to allow her position to expire with it. The CO-OP movement was thus truncated, its champion at CMS was eliminated, and the twenty-three CO-OPs under contract were basically left to fend for themselves when CMS replaced the highly regarded Smith with a junior-level staffer from another section of the agency.

To add to the confusion, no real goals were set that would constitute success for an individual CO-OP or the program as a whole. Aside from the overall aim of CO-OPs eventually repaying their loans, no metrics were developed by CMS (such as enrollment, patient outcomes, customer satisfaction, or effects on premiums in state markets with CO-OPs) that might have been used to promote or defend CO-OPs to a potentially hostile Congress.

With the funding appropriated for the CO-OP program, applicants for a statewide CO-OP could ask for both startup loans and solvency loans. Startup loan funds could be used to hire staff for the fledgling insurance companies, set up information technology systems, and pay for important activities of insurance, such as billing and claims payments. The latter, the "guts" of an insurance company, were outsourced by virtually all the original CO-OPs, which lacked the time and resources needed to undertake these crucial but labor-intensive operations before going live in the marketplace.

Solvency loans could only be used for reserves, the funds required by law to be held in abeyance by each insurance carrier (company) to cover any unexpected losses. Naturally, the amount of solvency funds needed increases as enrollment increases, and each state has its own requirements for how much solvency is required to stay off their "watch list." This requirement is known as risk-based capital (RBC), which is calculated by a complicated formula and comes out as a percentage. Most states require an RBC of 200% to be considered healthy. However, CMS, the agency charged with overseeing the entire Affordable Care Act, including the CO-OP program, arbitrarily chose 500% as the RBC to which they would hold the CO-OPs. Ostensibly, this was to provide greater protection to the investors in the CO-OPs—the taxpayers.

However, because an insurance carrier required more reserves as enrollment grew, this higher RBC requirement limited the enrollment of the CO-OPs, unless additional dollars were available to increase reserves. Unfortunately, since no additional federal funds were made available to the CO-OPs as a result of the "fiscal cliff" negotiations, and severe restrictions were imposed on an individual CO-OP's ability to raise outside capital, the ultimate ability of the individual CO-OPs to grow to a reasonable size looked gloomy.

Not knowing much of this at the time, early in 2010, a group of senior members of the Howard County Health Department, the county executive of Howard County, and I realized that some of the structure of the Healthy Howard Access Plan might be converted into something much more ambitious: Maryland's applicant to be a CO-OP. With encouragement from County Executive Ken Ulman, four of us from the Health Department leadership (Dawn O'Neill, the deputy health officer; Liddy Garcia-Buñuel, the executive director of Healthy Howard; Josh Curtis, the deputy director of Healthy Howard; and I, the Howard County health officer) began work on the application to become a CO-OP.

Dawn O'Neill had been my right-hand person throughout my professional life. First, serving as my chief of staff while I was the Baltimore City health commissioner, then as my campaign manager when I ran for the US Congress, and as the deputy health officer when I was the Howard County health officer. A native of Rochester, New York, with a kind, effusive personality, she knew me better than anyone outside my family, quirks and all. Without a doubt, I wanted her to come with me to work at our CO-OP.

Liddy Garcia-Buñuel was a forceful individual with strong opinions. Most of the time, we were in concert, but occasionally one of the four of us would have to call a truce. She had a wide-ranging public health background, having worked to get children signed up for healthcare in Seattle, before running the Healthy Howard Access Plan.

Josh Curtis has been one of our public policy interns at the Howard County Health Department. He was so impressive, with great organizational skills, that we hired him as the deputy director of Healthy Howard. Given his experience with that quasi-insurance entity, it made great sense to get him involved with our proposal and to bring him along to the CO-OP as well.

As all four of us lived in Baltimore, we decided to develop our proposal at a more convenient locale than Howard County, an hour south. The most central site was a small coffee shop in the Roland Park neighborhood of Baltimore City: the Evergreen Café. Over hours of discussion and debate, and drawing diagrams of the components of the CO-OP on napkins, the general form of the Maryland CO-OP, Evergreen Health Cooperative, slowly emerged.

We would seek licensure as a health maintenance organization, focusing on primary and preventive care for our members. We were all single payer advocates (indeed, I had run for Congress on just such a platform in 2006). We were not particularly interested in simply launching a CO-OP just to be a new insurance carrier in a stagnant marketplace. Instead, we viewed our insurance company as a vehicle (a single payer of sorts) to funnel as many of our members as possible to care at one of our planned primary care offices (PCOs).

We saw these PCOs as a way to implement healthcare reform the way many thought the ACA should have done. Our PCOs were based on three pillars, similar to healthcare reform guru Dr. Robert Berwick's "Triple Aim" of healthcare reform: better health outcomes at lower cost and with higher patient satisfaction.

1. We would change the payment structure from the perversely incentivized fee-for-service system (which rewards providers for seeing more patients, ordering more tests, and performing more procedures), almost universally used in the United States, to a capitated system (which rewards providers for delivering better health outcomes for their patients). To accomplish this, our primary care providers would have a patient roster that was half the national average, thus ensur-

ing them the time to truly listen to their patients and to give them high-quality care.

2. Our PCO providers would practice evidence-based medicine—in other words, provide services, medication, and testing that studies have shown contribute to the health of the patient rather than the wealth of the provider or medical institution.

3. Our PCOs would provide comprehensive patient-centered primary care, including behavioral health services, personalized health coaching, and care coordination on site to attend to the patient's holistic care in one visit.

On the insurance side, as well, we wanted to reform the system. Responding to complaints of friends and colleagues about their frustrations dealing with large insurance companies, we explicitly planned our customer service to be personalized and timely. Forty-five minute waits to talk to a representative of Evergreen would not be acceptable. Nor were rude or unknowledgeable customer representatives. To ensure these features, we would constantly monitor the calls of our reps for both tone and knowledge of our policies, and check wait times daily.

Our application to CMS laid out our innovative proposal:

> For any healthcare system to be successful, people must have both comprehensive insurance coverage as well as providers who can deliver patient-centered care. To have just good insurance with perfunctory care, or stellar doctors with unaffordable rates, is not enough if we want to improve health outcomes and decrease health system costs. The Evergreen vision is to integrate these two traditionally adversarial functions to ensure that members can access the full range of necessary healthcare services.

After several months of planning and discussion, we submitted our application to CMS in March 2012. Shortly thereafter we were told to come to Washington to present our proposal to members of the outside consulting firm Deloitte, which was contracted by CMS to vet the various proposals. The interview was relatively innocuous, and we left Washington fairly confident that our application would be approved. However, months went by without any word, while several CO-OPs were approved for operation in other states. Eventually, we heard back: our score was too low; the financials didn't seem to work. We were devastated, each of us having spent hundreds of hours on the application. I called the head of the CO-OP program at CMS, Barbara Smith, for guidance on whether reapplying made any sense. She suggested that we reexamine some of our assumptions about enrollment and rework our financial projections, but gave us little encouragement about the potential for a successful resubmission.

Dawn, Liddy, and Josh felt this was the end of our journey, but I wasn't ready to give up. Because I saw this as a real opportunity to be at the front line of health reform in the country, I refused to throw in the towel. Encouraged by my newfound hopeful energy—completely unsupported by the evidence— our team set to the task. We made the changes recommended by CMS and by September 2012, our second application was ready to be submitted.

Unfortunately, CMS did not value the innovative combined CO-OP/PCO concept as much as we did. Indeed, in response to our application including the PCOs, CMS changed the guidelines for all CO-OP applications at the tail end of the process to explicitly prohibit the use of federal funds for any clinical services, thus eliminating a key innovative portion of our proposed healthcare system. No reason was ever given for this sudden change.

Facing this last-minute obstacle to an otherwise potentially successful reapplication, we had to decide whether to proceed with the CO-OP without the PCO system. Reasoning that we could potentially add the PCO component down the road, I called CMS to inform them that we would move forward without the PCOs. Expecting a quick affirmative acknowledgment, I was extremely surprised to hear that they would now only approve our CO-OP application if the PCOs were included and we had confirmation of outside funding to stand up the offices. This was a brand-new requirement, even though they would not allow funding of the PCOs with federal dollars. As it was mid-September 2012, and the runway to a successful launch of the CO-OP was expected to take at least a year and a half, we were now up against a significant time crunch to be ready to go live on January 1, 2014. To obtain financing for the PCOs, I turned to three major foundations in the Baltimore metro area—the Abell Foundation, the Open Society Institute, and the Annie E. Casey Foundation—with whom I had good relationships from my days as Baltimore City health commissioner. I described our model and what made it unique: Evergreen Health would be one of the only organizations in the country with an integrated model of an insurance company with patient care offices that were developed with a vision of collaboration between coverage and care.

I also let the foundations know that the population we were striving to serve—those lower-income individuals and families who, with the passage of the ACA, would now be eligible for affordable health coverage—was the target population that the foundations desired to assist.

The entreaties were successful, resulting shortly thereafter in letters of intent from the three foundations that satisfied CMS. On September 27, we were officially awarded the CO-OP franchise for Maryland, and the accompanying $65.2 million in federal loans to implement it: $52.3 million for the legally required reserves and $12.9 million for startup costs, such as rent, staff, actuarial work, and claims-paying services.

With the money and a contract from the federal government in hand, I stepped down as Howard County health officer to become, on October 12, 2012, the first employee of the first new commercial health insurance company in Maryland in decades. Over the next month, my three Howard Health colleagues and cofounders joined me.

Taking into account our backgrounds, it made sense for Dawn to assume the chief operating officer position; Liddy (with her experience in the quasi-insurance Healthy Howard program) became chief of insurance; Josh, the director of operations; and I took on the role of CEO.

Working out of two rented offices at the top of a high-rise building in Towson, the town contiguous to Baltimore City's northern border, together we enthusiastically started working on a variety of tasks. Dawn and Liddy found payroll services, bought furniture and made plans for expansion. Josh worked on getting and connecting computers and setting up our financial record system. I spent most of my time developing the plans for launching the PCOs. It was exciting to be building something from the ground up, and very fulfilling to be working toward our goal of providing our own brand of healthcare reform to our fellow Marylanders.

For the first few months, almost daily, the four of us came together to screen and interview applicants for several crucial positions we needed to fill to accomplish the urgent tasks associated with filing for our insurance license in time to offer our still-to-be-developed insurance policies on the newly minted Maryland Health Benefit Exchange (the mechanism set up by the ACA to enable those without workplace-provided insurance to apply for individual policies, often with a federal subsidy).

We quickly added a chief financial officer and a chief compliance officer—both of whom came with previous insurance experience, in contrast to the original four members of the Evergreen staff. As we continued to grow over the ensuing few months, with a receptionist, a communications director, interns from the class I taught at Johns Hopkins, and our two initial PCO leaders, we rented several more rooms on the top floor of our building, eventually filling more than half of the floor with Evergreen staff.

Meanwhile, we all chipped in to answer questionnaires, provide detailed financial disclosures, and furnish other evidence that we could provide the services needed to be performed by a health insurer. In short order, we were able to show the state that we met all the requirements to obtain an insurance license, literally on the March 31 deadline. However, the Maryland insurance commissioner was out of the office that day and did not want to come back to sign the license. Taken aback, particularly since her boss, Gov. Martin O'Malley (I had served as his health commissioner for seven years), had made support for the ACA a priority, I fired off a quick email to Commissioner Goldsmith with a "loud cc" to Governor O'Malley and his chief of staff. The missive made it quite clear that the lack of an insurance license for Evergreen would result in the loss of lower-cost policies to previously uninsured Marylanders, which would be a travesty—and wouldn't look good for the O'Malley administration. Within ten minutes, a copy of our newly minted state insurance license came in over our fax line.

Chapter Two

A Rocky Start

April 2013 to March 2014

As we set about putting together an operating health insurance company with actual policies for real people, naysayers abounded. Brokers didn't express any interest in selling our products, and employers didn't want to take a chance on offering us to their employees. The state insurance commissioner expressed little support. Even health reform advocates strongly encouraged us not to even try to join the insurance market. As for the existing health insurance company executives, we weren't even gnats on their windshields, barely registering as a competitor.

Had we known how difficult it was to become a new health insurer, we might never have started Evergreen. The market was dominated by the region's Blue Cross/Blue Shield affiliate CareFirst, which effectively allowed them to set premiums at whatever level they wished. For example, they could underprice the competition to gain enrollment in one sector of the market and cover the temporary losses in that sector with profits in another sector. Additionally, CareFirst's dominance led to their control over the all-important broker community. In Maryland, small group (two to fifty employees) and large group business is largely controlled by insurance brokers, who make money by receiving commissions from the insurance companies whose policies they are selling. CareFirst, through its financial heft, was able to pay more to brokers with a variety of sweeteners, including retention bonuses (paid for keeping business with CareFirst) and resumption bonuses (paid for bringing back business lost by CareFirst). However, at the outset we had little knowledge of the odds that were stacked against Evergreen. Thinking back, there not having been another new commercial health insurer in Maryland in more than twenty-five years might have tipped us off.

As the summer of 2013 arrived, we took on the major tasks that we needed to complete in order to be ready for the first open enrollment period under the newly implemented Affordable Care Act. Since we were an organization of fewer than a dozen employees, compared to the big insurance carriers with thousands, there were several major areas of operations that we had to outsource (paying claims, sending bills, and preauthorizing services). Conveniently, there were several such entities around the country, called third-party administrators (TPAs), which would perform these "back office" services for a substantial fee. We chose a benefit consultant company to help us manage the process of vetting potential TPAs.

With few of us having any insurance experience, and the others mainly having worked with the much-different Medicaid system (care for impoverished citizens), we had literally no idea how to interpret the reports prepared for us on each TPA's proposal by the consultant. It basically came down to trusting his recommendation that we go with the local candidate (which I'll call "Care Solutions") over national entities, such as Xerox. As it turned out, this decision would be the worst move we made in the first three years of our operations. Care Solutions proved unable to gather even simple data about the health of our members, and its woefully inadequate technology was unable to collect all the data that was required by the ACA. Thus, our relationship with this TPA cost us dearly in time, money, stress, and reputation, until we eventually extricated ourselves early in 2016.

We then had to develop our insurance products that we would be offering in the marketplace. Under the ACA, individuals in Maryland without coverage through their employer could apply for individual coverage via the Maryland Health Benefits Exchange (Maryland was one of seventeen states that ran their own exchange; the rest of the states used the federal exchange), starting on October 1, 2013, for a January 1, 2014, effective date. To compete on the exchange for the individual market, Evergreen had to have a variety of types of insurance plans, priced so that they would be at least modestly competitive. With the overall lack of insurance experience among our tiny team, combined with our having no idea of the health or needs of our potential clients, we had little to go on, so we did what any untrained group would do in this situation—we looked to our competitor's plans and, to a large extent, copied them! This allowed us to have plans that were generally acceptable to consumers in our initial year of operation.

As we gained knowledge, we would eventually design innovative policies that would specifically address the needs of those with chronic conditions, for example, diabetes. Such a plan, termed a value-based policy, would provide all services that have been proven by studies to reverse diabetic severity to a customer at no out-of-pocket expense to the patient. So, for example, a diabetic patient with our value-based policy would receive insulin, glucose strips, Hemoglobin A1C tests (a blood test that measures long-term glucose control), foot doctor visits, endocrinologist visits, and primary care visits at no additional cost, not even a copay. The point of these policies was to remove any financial barriers to the diabetic patient's obtaining the care that studies have shown reduce complications of diabetes. By reducing the likelihood of hospitalizations for diabetic ketoacidosis or below-the-knee amputations, Evergreen's policies not only kept the patient healthier but also cost us less. These lower costs for our most common type of high-cost user led to lower premiums, as well. That was the type of innovative healthcare the ACA envisioned with new competitors like the CO-OPs.

Why had we hired virtually no staff with any insurance experience? The reason was simple: the section of the ACA that enabled the formation of the CO-OPs explicitly prohibited the involvement of board members and founders of these organizations to have health insurance carrier experience. The reason for this prohibition was to encourage a new type of member-centric insurance company. However noble the intention, the result was a cohort of carriers entering their respective state insurance markets with both hands tied behind their backs—lacking any name recognition in an industry where enrollees wanted to have comfort knowing that their healthcare was managed by a known quantity, all the while being run by inexperienced executives. No wonder over 80% of the initial CO-OPs would fail within three years!

To be frank, even without these restrictions, we would probably have opted for at least some of the staff to be hired from the nonprofit or public service world. Evergreen's founders all came from the public health arena and had strong negative feelings toward the existing health insurance system. Indeed, several of us strongly supported a single-payer system (sometimes called Medicare for All), in which all funding to cover healthcare is provided by the public sector, while providers in the private sector deliver care. To us, this seemed a much more equitable and less expensive arrangement than the incredibly complex and fragmented healthcare structure that exists in the United States. Our overwhelming desire to create an entirely new type of nonprofit, member-friendly insurance company dedicated to members, not profits, led us to choose like-minded individuals for our staff.

Insurance plans in hand, we turned them over to Milliman, our contracted actuarial firm, to determine appropriate pricing for our products. When they came back with proposed rates, based on analysis they had done on the population in Maryland, they estimated that Evergreen's plans would be among the lowest priced of all plans offered by the five insurance carriers participating in the first year of the Maryland exchange. However, Maryland's health insurance world worked in mysterious ways. Each insurance company files its proposed premiums (for each plan it offers) to the Maryland Insurance Administration (MIA) on May 1 of a given year. The MIA may approve those rates, or, over the next few months, go back and forth with the insurance company over what the proper rates should be if the MIA staff feels that the rates were not appropriately aligned with the risk of the projected population of clients.

In late August 2013, the MIA released the rates that would go into effect in the upcoming year for all plans by all carriers at the same time. No negotiations were allowed; what you got is what you had to sell for the entire open enrollment period.

Looking forward to being able to announce low premiums as we launched on the exchange, we were shocked to read the press release from the MIA: CareFirst had by far the lowest rates on the Maryland exchange. This was a conscious decision on their part. By significantly underpricing the individual market on the exchange (a loss they could cover with profits from other business lines), CareFirst hoped to capture such a large share of the individual market that they would knock out one or more of their smaller competitors right out of the gate. With less competition they would then raise premiums for these policies the following year to provide better financial results. In fact, eighteen plans from multiple insurers had lower premiums than Evergreen.

Never mind that our plans were more comprehensive, with lower deductibles than many of those plans—in other words, our plans had lower total out-of-pocket expenses than many of the low-premium high-deductible plans. However, none of that showed up on the exchange website. All the shoppers on the site could see was the cost of the premium for each plan. This, combined with CareFirst's near-universal name and brand recognition, put us in a real predicament. By so underpricing the market, CareFirst ended up getting more than 94% of the individuals from Maryland's exchange.

With this pricing debacle, we weren't sure we'd get more than a couple of thousand Marylanders to enroll with us, which very well might doom the CO-OP only months after launching. In fact, we did even worse—after six months of open enrollment, which was extended to March 31, 2014, due in part to the disastrously dysfunctional Maryland Health Benefit Exchange (described below), we had enrolled only a little over four hundred members.

Complicating matters in the lead-up to Evergreen's first year of operations as a nonprofit health insurance cooperative, we were also launching another startup. Parallel to bringing the CO-OP insurance products to market, we were also bringing the PCOs online, to be ready to serve our first enrollees who wanted to use them as their primary care provider, starting on January 1, 2014. Although the two organizations—Evergreen CO-OP and the PCOs—were technically separate entities, all of our CO-OP staff, and myself in particular, were deeply involved in launching the PCOs. But, before we could start working seriously on the nuts and bolts of building out four brand-new PCOs, we had to raise the funds needed to both build the centers and pay for operating expenses for at least a few years, until they could become cash-flow positive.

To do that, I turned again to the three foundations that had signed letters of intent when we submitted our final application to CMS. Needing $6 million for the project, we met jointly in early January 2013 with the three foundation presidents—Bob Embry at the Abell Foundation, Diana Morris at the Open Society Institute (a branch of the Open Society Foundation, funded by George Soros), and Patrick McCarthy at the Annie E. Casey Foundation. All three were very supportive, and expressed great faith in our motives and in our plans to use these centers to provide a truly revolutionary type of care to our target population. Each took the request to their boards—I presented telephonically to the OSF board in New York, after which George Soros chimed in that he would personally guarantee the OSI segment of the loan.

After each foundation had responded affirmatively, they got together as a group with legal counsel to work out the terms of the loan. It would be a line of credit with M&T Bank, which would allow us to draw down up to $6 million as needed. Casey guaranteed 40%, OSI 35%, and Abell 25%, with interest payments of 3%. The loan would have to be repaid after five years. With no problem, the terms were agreed to and $6 million became available for the use of the new nonprofit organization, Evergreen Health Care, which would run the PCOs.

I had set a firm goal that we have the four PCOs ready for patients on the first day Evergreen CO-OP could begin paying for care: January 1, 2014. However, when the PCO organization was set up in April of 2013, the PCOs' small initial staff of two—Jessica Kohnen and Liz Burger, along with our operations head, Josh Curtis—pushed back. They forcefully argued that we would never be able to stand up all four PCOs by the first of the year. It would be a huge task to build the spaces out, outfit the PCOs with equipment and furniture, and hire staff to cover them five days a week—in less than eight months.

Having known all three of my colleagues for years (Josh as a former intern and staffer at Healthy Howard; Jessica as a director of a nonprofit organization in Baltimore while I was health commissioner; and Liz as an extremely competent former middle and high school classmate of my eldest daughter, who had moved back to town after a management consultant stint in New York), I was particularly exasperated at what I perceived as unnecessary resistance. I called an all-staff meeting of Evergreen and the PCOs in the glass-enclosed conference room in our rented quarters on the top floor of the suburban office building. I was frustrated, because the existence of the PCOs was imperative to fulfilling the Evergreen mission—to align an insurer with a system of robust patient-centered medical homes, to better serve our members. By delaying the implementation of the PCOs, our vision would be incomplete.

Normally very even-keeled, I raised my voice for the first time in the several months of our efforts, making it clear that failure was not an option and storming out. Taken aback, the three quietly got to work and, to their great credit, got the sites open on time. They also signed on a great team of providers and staff and developed a system of care that received rave reviews from virtually all our patients.

Before the sites could open, of course, we had to find appropriate locations. To do so, we combed through demographic data down to the level of census tracts (considerably smaller populations than those found in a zip code), on population, average household income, and common occupations. We needed a substantial population of some 300,000 individuals within a radius of about twenty miles in order to provide us with an adequate-sized pool of potential patients for each PCO. Our goal was to serve 2,500 members per center, allowing for a far smaller patient panel per provider than average in Maryland, which would result in more time spent with each patient and more personalized care. A significant number of these individuals had to be living below 400% of the federal poverty level ($95,000 for a family of four), which would allow them to be eligible for a subsidized insurance policy on the exchange and therefore to choose Evergreen. Finally, we wanted to pick areas with high levels of workers in occupations less likely to provide insurance and therefore less likely to have previous access to a primary care provider. In other words, we wanted to pick areas with large numbers of lawn service or restaurant employees, for example, who might choose Evergreen insurance because it would give them access to the comprehensive primary care that would be available at our PCOs. I spent countless hours driving up and down the I-95 corridor with our realtor David Paulson and the executive director of the PCOs, Jessica Kohnen, looking at potential sites for our care centers.

Our travels to find suitable buildings for the centers had their humorous moments, as the current use for a given location was not necessarily disclosed in the commercial real estate listings that Paulson had obtained. Thus, on a trip to a site in downtown Baltimore, we found a building with a labyrinthine assortment of rooms, many filled with old medical devices, that looked as if the owners had gone bankrupt and left everything they had right where it was. But the visit that took the cake was when we went to a workmanlike commercial district in Glen Burnie, just south of Baltimore. After rechecking the listing to confirm that the address was correct, we found ourselves staring at a site that shared a front with a shop selling sex toys and adult movies. Figuring such a location would not sit well with many of our patients, we moved on.

By August of 2013 we had chosen our sites: White Marsh, at a location across the street from a major shopping mall in Baltimore County, in the middle of a vast area of working- and middle-class population; the Rotunda, a soon-to-be-redeveloped shopping center and residence, located in a socio-economically and racially mixed area of Baltimore City; Columbia, in a typically nondescript building in this large planned town in Howard County; and Greenbelt, in a nice high-rise medical office building in a community in Prince George's County, near Washington, with a sizable population of working- and middle-class families and a growing number of Hispanic residents.

With the sites chosen, Josh went to work with the architects to design and outfit the centers. I recommended a "Starbucksian" feel of soothing dark colors and softer lighting—as opposed to the typical bright clinical lighting and putrid green paint found in many medical offices. The patient rooms and the layout of the centers were designed to have the patient remain in one room for the entire visit, while the relevant staff came to see the patient in their room. Josh and the team did a phenomenal job, turning out four truly patient-centered medical offices.

Indeed, our PCOs' focus on the previously mentioned "Triple Aim" of healthcare reform (greater patient satisfaction with care, with better health outcomes at lower cost) led to truly exceptional services for members of the centers. The following three comments from three patients are representative of the literally hundreds of reviews the PCOs received.

> I just wanted to say that the White Marsh office was the best doctor's office I've ever had. Dr. S. and Sara were awesome. The team made me feel relaxed and like I mattered to them: not just a number to fill a spot like every other office. If every doctor's office was run that way, the world would be a much better place.

> This experience was so different from any sort of healthcare that I've received. I'm blown away. Comprehensive and personal—very different from the healthcare I thought was available to me in my price range.

> This place is extraordinary. I've never had a doctor's visit so comprehensive and compassionate. This is what healthcare should be: supportive care with expert professionals of different disciplines in one beautiful place!

When we needed to start getting our name out prior to the first open enrollment period in late 2013, I felt that—in contrast to our lack of experience about commercial insurance—at least in this area we had some real-world experience with marketing. Dawn O'Neill and I had managed a $750,000 advertising budget during my campaign for Congress in 2006—a campaign that won wide praise for the effectiveness of both its television and print ads. The consultant responsible for the advertising, Jim Crounse, was a great guy, who had stayed in contact with Dawn and me over the next several years. When we approached him about working with us, he immediately signed on. However, because there was a prohibition on using federal loan funds for advertising, we had to be very careful to couch our efforts as an educational campaign about the benefits of the ACA and having a new competitor in the marketplace.

Having mentored Jim Messina, President Obama's former deputy chief of staff and the manager for the president's 2012 reelection campaign, Crounse wanted to implement some of the most up-to-date data analytical techniques used by the president's campaign. He brought Messina to meet with me in the spring of 2013 at the Hilton Baltimore BWI Airport hotel. Admittedly nervous to meet this famous political figure, I was struck by how unpretentious and down to earth he was from the get-go (and how often he cursed). Listening to our philosophy of healthcare and mission, he was particularly struck by the idea of our planned PCOs. He was also a very quick study. Of course, he knew a fair amount about the ACA from his time in the White House, during the legislative fight to enact the ACA, but he rapidly understood the nuances of the CO-OP program and our specific innovative plans for Evergreen.

Although prohibited from using our startup federal funds for advertising per se, we still wanted to know what features of Evergreen would resonate with Marylanders. To that end, we first held focus groups with individuals from diverse demographic sectors—gender, race, location within Maryland, insured/uninsured, Democrat/Republican/Independent. We had four such groups (run by David Binder, who had run focus groups for the president's campaign all over the country). We spent a lot of time beforehand with the facilitator on questions to be asked and terms to be used. We wanted to get as good an idea as possible about which messages were likeliest to motivate different groups to buy our insurance.

We tested whether being a cooperative was a differentiator—no, it wasn't. Did support for the president and Obamacare encourage someone to buy Evergreen as a product of the ACA?—yes, modestly. Did Evergreen being new, vastly less known, and much smaller than the big insurers like Care-First negatively influence potential buyers?—not really. Did the idea of the PCOs influence folks?—yes, particularly if they didn't have a regular primary care physician. They even tested if seeing me associated with the company influenced potential customers—a bit, but only in the Baltimore region. So, what really motivated these dozens of focus group participants? Cost, plain and simple. If our premiums were the lowest or among the lowest, the clear majority of participants would be willing to take a chance on a new entity.

With information in hand, Crounse and company got to work on a series of educational print pieces and a television spot. Meanwhile, Messina hired Civis—the data analytic team that had produced such an unexpected benefit to the Obama campaign in 2012—to identify those residents of the state who would most likely fit the demographics that would use the exchange (prior to the crash of the Maryland exchange coming out of the gate, our original target population was primarily those who would qualify for subsidies on the exchange). Since we were hamstrung by the insurance lobby amendment to the CO-OP section of the ACA, which prohibited the use of any of our startup loan for advertising, once individuals were identified, the plan was to go from door to door, campaign-style, to educate them about Evergreen's philosophy and the availability of a new form of health insurance.

To get workers for the door-to-door effort, we turned to yet another participant in the Obama campaign, Sheila O'Connell. After we described the message we wanted her to present, she quickly gathered a crew of individuals with campaign outreach experience. Various Evergreen staff presented information to the workers during their training period and then, with printed material in hand, the outreach staff went into the community.

Because only licensed insurance brokers in Maryland can talk to individuals about insurance premiums and benefits, we made it explicit to our outreach workers that any discussion of plan specifics was forbidden. Within a few weeks, the outreach effort had hit several thousand doors with printed educational material that was focused solely on providing information on the ACA and how to access the Maryland exchange. At the bottom of the handout was a tear-off that could be mailed back with the individual's contact information, so that licensed brokers at Evergreen could reach out to them with information about our policies and potentially help them enroll. The outreach effort was a bit less effective than expected, yielding a few hundred returned requests for information. To reach out to those who had expressed interest, we had a "call night," when the entire staff at Evergreen (about thirty strong by the summer of 2013) made calls to virtually all the interested individuals over the course of a single evening.

Amazingly, although the results of the outreach campaign were modest, our behemoth of a competitor, CareFirst, felt threatened enough to file a complaint about our campaign with the Maryland Insurance Administration, claiming that the outreach workers were soliciting business without an insurance license. To our dismay, the O'Malley administration's insurance commissioner told us to shut the effort down, even though we had made it clear to her that the staff had explicit instructions on what they could or could not say to individuals at their door and were only educating consumers about the new era of health insurance under the ACA. In retrospect, the MIA decision was probably correct—it just felt at the time that we deserved a break, considering the limitations that were placed on us to get the word out about Evergreen.

Shutting down the community-based campaign left us primarily with our educational infomercial as Evergreen's sole introduction to potential consumers. We had to be very careful about how we talked about Evergreen to avoid the spot being defined as an advertisement. The piece that Jim Crounse and his colleagues produced was very professional and focused primarily on some introductory comments about the Evergreen philosophy and on the Evergreen PCOs as a potential sales advantage in the market. I thought they were great, but some of the others on our staff thought they focused too much on the PCOs, which might confuse consumers into thinking that we were actually a string of urgent care centers. The proof of the effectiveness of the television spot would have been in the outcome of open enrollment, but the disastrous rollout of the Maryland exchange at the end of 2013 precluded any conclusions on the matter.

One outcome from the marketing effort of our first open enrollment period was some conflict between some senior staff and me about the value of our various consultants. They were concerned that we spent far too much on the effort, for far too little in results. As noted, I think it was impossible to tell how effective the effort would have been because of external circumstances beyond our control. On the former point, they were probably right— my excitement at having these political stars working with us did color my thoughts to some extent. You live and you learn—the next year's marketing effort would be very different.

Intent on never becoming a stodgy corporate insurance company, we set out to intentionally develop a collaborative, supportive organizational culture. To that end, group activities and team-building efforts were frequent occurrences. (I remember an exercise in which we all had to throw oranges to each other, though I can't remember the point of it.) Although the original organizational culture was a bit too touchy-feely for my taste, because the intent was good and this was a CO-OP, after all, it was important that the staff be able to propose certain initiatives—and the team-building exercises provided a sense of camaraderie for many of our original contingent of staff.

The most successful project growing out of the attempt to develop a unique inclusive organizational culture was the effort to find a suitable headquarters building. Josh Curtis was tasked with finding the company's permanent home. Knowing that we preferred a distinctive, cool-looking headquarters, after a fair amount of exploration the search boiled down to three buildings, all about the same rent per square foot: a suburban medical professional building; a wrought-iron-fronted five-story historic office building in downtown Baltimore, near the Baltimore Orioles' ballpark at Camden Yards; and an old reconstructed cotton mill in the eclectic Hampden area of Baltimore, on the Jones Falls (a river running through Baltimore). The first was ruled out as too generic; the second had logistical problems; the third was perfect.

The layout of the office space was based on the open-floor model used in my daughter Jane's workplace in Washington, DC. Impressed by the sense of collaboration I felt when visiting her office, we incorporated several elements of that company's space in Evergreen's home. There were lots of glass-windowed conference rooms, as well as cooperative spaces, like our "living rooms" (open spaces with couches and low tables, overlooking the fast-flowing Jones Falls) and two large kitchen/common eating spaces. In addition, we had very few actual offices, preferring that teams work in open spaces near each other to allow for more interaction. Josh did a wonderful job bringing the idea to reality—I never heard a visitor to our headquarters who didn't comment on the building and its setting. More than any other concrete aspect of Evergreen, the character of our main building defined the Evergreen culture. Indeed, it always brightened my day to walk through the old mill building and peer through the glass at our dedicated staff working across division lines, attacking the problem of the day.

While the trials and tribulations of the federal exchange were widely discussed and used to diminish the president and his signature policy, several states that chose to run their own exchanges suffered even greater problems. Unfortunately for Evergreen, one of them was Maryland. Because Gov. Martin O'Malley saw the exchange as a potential boon to his long-planned candidacy for the presidency in 2016, Maryland was the first state to be granted the ability to develop its own exchange.

A brief description of an exchange is in order. The exchanges (both the federally run exchange in thirty-plus states, and the exchanges run by seventeen states) are basically online shopping sites for health insurance policies, somewhat analogous to travel websites, like Expedia and Travelocity (though far more complicated and nuanced). Individuals who were not offered affordable coverage through their employer or were self-employed entered demographic details about themselves and their family members, including age, gender, and family income into the exchange's online application system. Those with incomes below 400% of the federal poverty level (about $95,000 for a family of four in 2014), but above the Medicaid-eligible level of 138% of the poverty level (about $33,000 for a family of four in 2014), qualified for a graduated federal subsidy, which could be applied to the premium costs of the various healthcare policies that popped up on the screen. This sounds simple enough: just find a plan with premiums that are affordable with the aid of a federal subsidy, click on it, and you're enrolled. Right? Wrong. The offerings were actually extremely complicated, and the websites did not offer much more information than the sticker price—that is, the monthly premium.

The specific plans are complicated because they are categorized in one of four metal levels—bronze, silver, gold, and platinum. Each of the plans covers different benefits and different percentages of the overall cost of a plan, depending on the metal level. Complicating the matter further is the way in which members are responsible for paying for services. In health insurance, the total costs to a plan member are not just the premium, which can be the least costly component. It is extremely important to know the deductible (how much members must pay themselves, before their insurance kicks in). Oftentimes, a low premium means you have a very high deductible (as high as $7,000 per person). Similarly, one must consider the copays (the set fee you pay to a provider at each visit) and coinsurance (the percentage of a bill you are responsible for). The biggest problem with the exchange system was the lack of transparency into the true cost of a plan—it took three years after the initial implementation of the ACA for some of this information to become available to consumers on most exchanges.

Even though Maryland's initial exchange provided little information to prospective consumers (presumably making it simpler to design), it failed miserably. From the first day, the Maryland Health Benefit Exchange was open, October 1, 2013, virtually no one could access the site, let alone actually enroll.

The failure of the Maryland exchange was terribly distressing to the leadership of Evergreen, both for the damage it did to our business plan, and because it prevented many tens of thousands of working- and middle-class Marylanders—those for whom we had started the CO-OP—from obtaining health coverage they desperately hoped for. In a blue state, with tremendous support for the ACA and with significant state resources devoted to developing the Maryland exchange, how did it fail so badly?

Members of our staff who attended weekly exchange-carrier meetings in the summer of 2013 raised the first hint of trouble. As the summer went on they told me of their concerns that finalizing the exchange's processes and rules was taking too long and that there would not be enough time to test the exchange's functionality before going live on October 1. We relayed these concerns to the exchange staff numerous times over the next couple of months. Indeed, we even offered to help test the "shopping experience" on the testing platform, but were turned down. Not being privy to the actual deliberations and discussion by the operators and overseers of the exchange, we had no idea how poorly the rollout would go.

On opening day, the exchange crashed coming out of the gate. As the first week went on, we were continuously reassured by the powers-that-be that the glitches would be fixed quickly. By the next week, that clearly not being the case, several of us at Evergreen started testing the functionality of the different parts of the exchange. We hoped to relay specific glitches to the exchange, since the lack of pre-go-live testing meant that testing and fixes would have to be made on "a plane in flight rather than in a hangar."

In going on the exchange website 287 times during the period of October 10, 2013, to February 7, 2014, using different family members' names, for whom I had social security numbers, I got stuck in the exchange process everywhere from registering my account, giving a password, starting the shopping experience, choosing my health status, seeing the cost of a premium on a plan, choosing a plan, and hitting the enrollment button. Each of these obstacles was reported to the exchange—often with no improvement. On the one time I made it through the entire process, and enrolled, that enrollment was recorded as multiple enrollments by the same individual in the same plan—

that is, I was enrolled eight times in the same plan—something that was obviously not supposed to happen.

Some of these glitches improved over the next few months, but the experience of navigating the exchange was still burdensome and the premium calculation suspect. We at Evergreen recommended that anyone wanting a subsidy via the exchange go directly to a navigator entity (locality-based staff funded by the exchange to guide individuals through the application process). Our rationale was based on discussions with navigators, all of whom knew the best workarounds to bypass online obstacles. They were completing the process about 50%–80% of the time, although often taking up to two hours to do so. The rate of successful navigation for an individual trying on his or her own was virtually nil.

Marylanders should not have had to endure this difficult process, even with help. The average person didn't have the time to spend slogging through the exchange—often several times—or the time to wait forty-five to seventy minutes for a call center representative to provide guidance. Due to these snafus, many were denied timely access to the health coverage and care to which they were entitled.

Since we at Evergreen knew that those whom we were mission-driven to serve were likely to need significantly more healthcare services than others, we developed plans that were focused more on copays than on huge deductibles. This meant that our plans were more comprehensive, more affordable, and consumer-friendlier than very-low-premium very-high-deductible policies. For our target group, whose members would mostly be classified either as having some health needs or as having significant health needs, our copay-focused plans meant that after they had covered the much lower Evergreen deductible, members were responsible for only modest copays of $25 to $50 per visit. Because of this our plans were often very competitive, if not the lowest in overall cost to the consumer.

However, all that showed up in the shopping experience on the Maryland exchange was the "sticker price"—the monthly premium. Thus, the entire first page of the exchange's policy offerings was dominated by low-premium policies with very high deductibles from our competitors. Because there was not disclosure of true costs, there ended up being thousands of very disappointed Maryland consumers who didn't realize that a policy with a $150 per month premium with a $6,000 deductible meant they would be out $7,800 before any insurance kicked in ($150 × 12 months = $1,800 premium + $6,000 deductible = $7,800). Indeed, close to 40% of individuals who enrolled with our chief competitor on the exchange for 2014 dropped their coverage by September, due to the perceived lack of benefit.

What was the bottom line from the disaster that was the first year of Maryland's exchange? A total of 65,000 individuals signed up on the exchange (about half the predicted number, even though open enrollment was expanded far beyond its original deadline)—85% with incomes low enough to make them eligible for federal subsidies to make premiums more affordable. The clear majority of these applicants chose less expensive premium plans with high deductibles, not knowing that these plans would not meet many of their needs. These types of plans were heavily marketed by CareFirst, the Maryland affiliate of Blue Cross / Blue Shield. As mentioned earlier, since all other carriers were significantly underpriced by CareFirst, it got 94% of the individual on-exchange market in the first year of ACA implementation. So much for increased competition in the marketplace.

Chapter Three

Gaining Experience

April 2014 to June 2015

With only 400 members by the end of open enrollment in March 2014, and virtually no further enrollment to come via the exchange (only those with life events like marriage could enroll outside the official open enrollment period), Evergreen was in dire straits. And, because our enrollment was a matter of public record, everyone knew it. We clearly could not survive the year with only a few hundred members.

In fact, we were the butt of jokes among the CO-OPs that obtained significant enrollments. It got so bad that on our regular NASHCO (National Alliance of State Health Cooperatives) conference calls between all the CO-OP CEOs around the country, the larger CO-OPs would openly discuss their plans to take over some of the smaller ones. Indeed, on one such call, the CEO of a low-enrolled CO-OP told the group that he had talked with the director of the CO-OP program at CMS, who told him such a discussion had been going on between CMS and the larger CO-OPs. The president of the CO-OP association initially denied this, then came clean and blamed the CMS staffer for disclosing that fact. What ensued was a bizarre discussion among this group, which was supposedly working for the good of all the CO-OPs, but was breaking into factions of predator and prey. The call ended when several small

CO-OP CEOs asked if they were on the list to be gobbled up by one of their compatriots, only to be told, one by one, that yes, they were.

Often mentioned as one of the CO-OPs poised to be taken over, we took action to increase our enrollment off the exchange. We quickly shifted gears after the failed rollout of the exchange and applied to the Maryland Insurance Administration (MIA) to be able to sell on the small group market as well. Small groups, defined as companies with fifty or fewer employees, tended to be a somewhat neglected market in Maryland. By the end of March, we were approved to sell to these groups, and with a few well-designed plans and a two-year rate-stability program, we took our small group products to the brokers who governed the small group marketplace. By offering competitively priced policies we could give the brokers increased relevance. For the first time in more than twenty years in Maryland, a new health insurer entered the marketplace, providing more value to the brokers as professionals in presenting the options to clients.

Entering the small group market was a game saver. By December 31, 2014, we had sold over a thousand group policies, netting over 11,000 enrollees, allowing us to finish our first year of operations with almost 12,000 members. Mind you, due to our small enrollment and the necessity of undertaking a range of expensive activities required of a fledgling insurance carrier, we still ran a deficit of about $16 million for the year. However, the late bump in enrollment bought us time to grow further and diversify in our second year.

Although hired in our early, fragile phase, our public relations director's efforts got us press that brought us into the national media as the most-reported-on representative of the CO-OP program (a presence not appreciated by several of the larger CO-OPs, at least while they still existed). Matt Jablow was a long-time television reporter with the local NBC affiliate, WBAL-TV. I had met him years earlier, when he often covered me while I was the Baltimore health commissioner. I had always had a friendly relationship with him—both as a reporter and later as the press secretary for the Baltimore Police Department, so I thought of him immediately as our director of public relations.

Matt had developed a vast set of national media connections over his career. Combined with my exposure in the local media market for more than twenty years, this led to a lot of coverage locally and nationally. Evergreen was, of course, frequently covered by the *Baltimore Sun* and Baltimore television, but also the *New York Times*, the *Wall Street Journal*, and the *Washington*

Post, as well as CBS National News and Bloomberg TV. Indeed, the host of Bloomberg Morning, Tom Kean, took to calling me an expert on the Affordable Care Act, leading to my regular appearances on the show—I even served as guest host on one occasion.

As is often the case, exposure, particularly in the national media, can be a two-edged sword. Since the stories about Evergreen were generally very favorable, it brought the company a lot of positive attention, but it also meant that we had a bigger target on our back for ACA opponents than the quieter CO-OPs.

Unfortunately, the failure of the Maryland insurance exchange also directly affected the viability of the PCOs. Why? Because the model of our entire CO-OP/PCO system envisioned the CO-OP funneling many of its members to the PCOs, where we could deliver care in a personalized and robust new way. But with only about 400 enrollees of the CO-OP by March 2014, enrollment at the PCOs was miniscule—a total of just over 100 patients across the four centers. With a staff of five for each center (a family physician, a nurse practitioner, a licensed clinical social worker / health coach, a medical assistant, and a care coordinator), the few patients we had got a phenomenal level of care, but clearly the situation was not sustainable. We were burning through cash with very little revenue from caring for our few patients.

Realizing that we had to increase our patient population, we considered a variety of options. Should we temporarily postpone our efforts at payment reform (capitation) and open our centers to members of other insurance companies as a site for their primary care on a fee-for-service basis? This didn't prove viable, as other carriers either refused to play ball with us or were willing to pay so little per visit that it wasn't cost-effective. We also investigated Medicare, but the process to become a Medicare provider for seniors was cumbersome and would be too lengthy to bear fruit in our time-sensitive situation.

So we turned to Medicaid (health coverage for impoverished individuals with the cost split between the federal and state governments). In Maryland, as in many states, Medicaid is primarily provided by MCOs—managed care organizations, which are similar to commercial insurance companies, with their own panel of providers. Mark Puente, the CEO of Riverside Health, a new Medicaid MCO, quickly agreed to work with us. He even agreed to capitated payment for each of his members who became part of one of the

PCO's panels. We approached two other Medicaid MCOs and were successful in contracting with them as well, albeit on a fee-for-service payment basis.

This approach brought us much-needed revenue to stanch the financial hemorrhage of the centers. But the biggest new revenue stream would come from an unlikely source for an unusual reason.

In May 2014, investigations by several national news sources revealed that dozens of health centers around the country run by the Veterans Health Administration (VHA) of the US Department of Veterans Affairs (VA) had huge wait times for veterans needing primary care and other services, leading to serious health consequences for many of those affected. We felt—as did many others—that it was an outrage for thousands of veterans to be unable to receive care for many months and that it was a travesty for many VHA centers across the country to have covered up this backlog. Congress expressed its displeasure, demanding that the VA system respond immediately to get needed care to these veterans stuck in the queue.

Because of our system of primary care offices, we were in a unique position to help address the problem in Maryland. We immediately reached out to the Maryland VHA (which had the fourth-worst average wait time for appointments in the entire country), letting them know that we had the capacity to provide same-day primary care visits to dozens of veterans each day. It seemed a win-win-win: our veterans could be given quality care quickly and in a comprehensive manner; the VHA's backlog could be significantly reduced; and Evergreen Health Care's PCOs would be reimbursed for the care it provided while serving a very important group of individuals. As a nonprofit entity, with no shareholders or investors, no one associated with Evergreen had anything financial to gain from this offer.

Easy solution to a big problem, right? Well, no. Months of absurd bureaucratic wrangling ensued as our offer went all the way up the VA chain of command to its chief legal counsel in Washington, delaying any progress. Even though we were assured by the national VA that a contract was imminent, had tremendous support from our US senator Ben Cardin, and had comments from the Maryland VHA executive team that our model was exactly what they wanted for their veterans, we were told by national VA officials that the process has been delayed because "there is a lot of public and congressional interest in this and we have to follow all federal regulations."

Since "federal regulations" obviously weren't followed in the self-inflicted

debacle in which the VA was embroiled, it seemed ironic that this bureaucratic excuse was offered up. Meanwhile, the hypothetical servicewoman who
had served in Afghanistan with undiagnosed depression or a Vietnam veteran
with untreated high blood pressure sat home awaiting care, although it was
just an approval away. Evergreen had no interest in being the sole provider
of primary care for veterans in Maryland—we simply wanted our veterans to
receive the care that they deserved.

The inability of the VA to provide timely care raises the obvious question:
Why have a separate VA health system in this country? There is a simple
alternative—provide veterans with a Medicare card. Under this plan, any veteran who now qualifies for services from the current VA would simply qualify
for Medicare. The benefits of this approach are manifold, but among the most
important are the following:

1. Instead of having to receive care at a limited number of sites throughout the country, as is currently the case for veterans served by the
   VA, veterans would have literally hundreds of thousands of providers
   willing and able to provide their care in their own community.
2. Medicare has very low administrative overhead, and the addition of
   millions more members would provide for even greater economies of
   scale.
3. Obviously, no longer running a parallel and often duplicative system
   of several hundred large VA hospitals and medical campuses would
   save significant federal dollars.

Some will argue that veterans deserve care tailored to their needs and that
only the VA can do that. That may be true for a very discrete set of conditions—
PTSD and combat-related injuries immediately come to mind—and for those
conditions, the VA might still oversee specialized centers for these very limited number of specialized diagnoses.

Others will argue, correctly, that the VA has been a source of a variety of
reforms and best practices—for instance, telemedicine, electronic medical
records, and negotiating lower pharmaceutical costs. Let's learn from their
good works, and implement them in the larger healthcare system.

Eventually, the VA did contract with Evergreen to provide care for Maryland veterans at our four PCOs. The VA trumpeted the partnership on local
TV and national media, and Evergreen delivered on our promise of compre-

hensive high-quality care delivered with virtually no wait for the approximately 500 veterans we served. Due to good collaboration with the Maryland VA medical leadership, kinks were worked out (mainly consisting of difficult connections with differing IT systems), and all parties seemed to be satisfied. The story of one veteran served by the PCOs and relayed by one of our administrators illustrates the benefits that Evergreen was able to provide for VA patients:

> This veteran, a gentleman in his fifties, was referred to an Evergreen PCO when he couldn't be seen in a timely manner at the Baltimore VA medical center. The patient had very poorly controlled Type II diabetes, was significantly overweight, and had foot issues, which made it difficult to exercise. He was given an appointment two days after requesting to be seen at our PCO. In the patient-centered comprehensive model of care we provided, he worked with the PCO physician, nurse practitioner, health coach, and care coordinator, receiving extensive dietary education, lifestyle modification training, and help with his foot condition, which allowed him to increase his physical activity. In a short period, he was eating in a much healthier manner, was physically active, and was regularly monitoring his blood sugar. Within three months, his diabetes was completely controlled *without* insulin.

This case and hundreds like it made it seem that the VA-Evergreen relationship was a success. But wait, the VA brass (now led by a new secretary, after the resignation of his predecessor owing to the care backlog) decided it wanted to cancel all community-based contracts like ours and bring all care back in-house. So, after a year of providing high quality service to our veterans, we transitioned their care back to the Maryland VA—and it is no surprise that the waits for care have risen rapidly ever since.

Reacting to our less-than-stellar enrollment on the exchange in 2013, and the general feeling that the first year's campaign focused too much on the PCOs, Evergreen's 2014 marketing campaign went in a different direction. Choosing a Philadelphia firm, Allen & Gerritsen (A&G), which produced very slick and creative ads, we revamped our message to being the cool and somewhat ironic new health insurance organization. By late in the year in 2014, we could market ourselves legally, because we now had millions of directly earned revenue from premiums that could pay for advertising, ameliorating the need to use precluded federal loan funds.

The television ads they produced were catchy and memorable. One featured a hip young African American man on a stoop and a Latino cook in a kitchen stressing our wide network of providers and personalized service ("call Evergreen Health to speak to a real live human being"). The spots were filmed in Boston—I'm not sure why—and much time was spent arguing with the A&G staff about the location they chose for the stoop shot. Baltimore front stoops and row-house architecture are much different from Boston's— for example, Baltimore has marble stoops; Boston has brick. We insisted that the shot be tight enough to keep the viewer from seeing that the stoops used in the ad were not marble. But aside from some conflicts over the shooting venue, we were very pleased with the ad, and we heard great reviews from friends and acquaintances about its appeal.

The second piece depicted a middle-class white couple sitting on their couch talking about Evergreen's vast network of providers and personalized service. Again, very well produced and catchy, and many viewers remembered the "wife's" long-drawn-out "vaaast" when describing Evergreen's network of providers.

Clearly the second ad campaign (2014) was very different from the first, not even mentioning the PCOs, which were the focus of our initial campaign. Still, we were able to add about 4,500 individual members to our rolls, and an additional 10,000 group members. However, if I had to say whether this increase in enrollment was due to our advertising approach or to more competitive pricing, I'd choose the latter.

Although we were generally pleased with the quality of the work, we had some difficulty working with A&G, partly over strategy, but mainly over their high cost and lack of communication, a result of their rare visits to Baltimore. We determined to choose our next ad agency with those issues in mind.

Unfortunately, the characteristics that make for great founders of a startup often don't translate into the traits necessary to run and grow the business. In our case, at Evergreen, this was compounded by the fact that none of the original leaders had any real experience with or knowledge of insurance. Although Evergreen's enrollment was improving, there were still significant concerns about our viability and, concurrently, that of the PCOs (since they depended almost exclusively on Evergreen CO-OP for their patients).

Since the foundations had over $6 million in guaranteed loans supporting the PCOs, in an attempt to protect their investment, at the end of 2014 they asked us to bring in several consultants to evaluate the operations of both the CO-OP and the PCOs. After their fairly critical reviews, it became clear that we needed to makes some changes in the leadership of Evergreen.

As the CEO, it fell to me to make the extremely difficult decision to let two of Evergreen's founders go. While I had a friendly and quite collegial relationship with Liddy, and laying her off was very distressing, releasing Dawn was tremendously painful. She had been at my side throughout all four of the positions I had held over the prior twenty years. During that time, she had been my most important advisor and had done a great job overseeing hundreds of employees and dozens of programs. While those organizational skills carried over successfully to her role as chief operating officer at Evergreen, it was clear that her understandable lack of insurance knowledge was impeding Evergreen's progress. So, at an ironic location—the Evergreen Café—I met with her in early 2015 to inform her of my decision. To her great credit, she handled the situation with tremendous grace, and thanks to her dignified response, we have remained good friends.

The pain of making these moves was compounded by a form of survivor guilt. Why should I—with a similar lack of insurance knowledge—be allowed to stay on, while two of the other founders were to be let go? There was no simple answer to this question. Would it make sense to search for a new CEO with insurance experience, and make me a sort of figurehead? Or should I step aside and leave the company? This possibility was not terribly disturbing, as, by this time, I was not enjoying the job anywhere near as much as my public health positions. Indeed, Chris, my wife, was very supportive of me making a change back to the public health arena. But in the end, the consensus among the consultants and our Board of Directors was that my departure would have bad optics. Since I was, to many, the "face of Evergreen," it was concluded that it would be too destabilizing to the company and send a negative message to the marketplace—so I continued as CEO and president of Evergreen.

Chapter Four

The Obstacles Pile Up

Summer 2015

One of our original decisions—our poorly informed choice of a third-party administrator—became one of the most significant problems of 2015, our second year of operation. It had become clear to us by early 2015 that our TPA—Care Solutions—was simply unable to perform a variety of routine duties. Although we had placed them on eight different corrective action plans, we had never really held their feet to the fire.

Having learned a lot of lessons during our ongoing building phase, as well as with the departure of some of our original leadership team, I made a concerted effort to bring in experienced insurance executives to our newly constituted senior leadership group. We brought on Susy Kreiskott, a no-nonsense straight shooter, who came with decades of experience in the commercial insurance arena, to take on provider relations and credentialing, to assure that the majority of our members' visits were to physicians with whom we had a direct contract, allowing us to better ensure the provision of high quality care. Rob Lord, a kind, even-keeled fellow, brought thirty years of insurance sales knowledge to head up our sales department, and Mary Porter came on as our general counsel after years of working in the regulatory aspects of the insurance field. Finally, we pulled Manny Sheldon away from his CFO position with a high-enrollment CO-OP to become our chief financial officer.

Manny Sheldon was a piece of work. A raconteur, he could be charming one minute and loudly abrasive the next. Very full of himself, but with significant financial experience in the insurance world, he pushed from the very beginning of his time at Evergreen to be given the title of COO and CFO. Shocked by his assertiveness, I informed him that we would wait and see how things worked out as CFO first.

As soon as Manny came on board in February 2015, he realized that the relationship with Care Solutions was irreparable. He took the lead on extricating us from this unsatisfactory relationship. Although the process would prove arduous, contentious, and often maddening, it was absolutely necessary for the success of Evergreen going forward.

Digging into the guts of the company's activities, he became convinced that we had largely been sold a bill of goods when it came to Care Solution's actual capabilities. Although this hadn't come out in the bidding process with our consultant, we found that Care Solutions had not previously functioned as a TPA for a commercial carrier like us, nor were they able to perform the tasks required of a TPA under the new rules of the Affordable Care Act. Sheldon found that they could pay claims, but little else—they couldn't provide the data we needed on medical trends with our members, nor could they give us live feeds on who our members actually were.

In March 2015, we notified Care Solutions that we were going to pursue a course of action to get out of the remainder of our original contract (which lasted until December 31, 2016), due to their inability to meet the terms of our contract. In a long-drawn-out legal battle, which eventually went to mediation, we finally came to a deal to extricate ourselves by the end of the year. In the meantime, however, our choice of this TPA would be quite damaging.

While hostilities were starting to brew between Care Solutions and Evergreen, a larger problem arose—one that would severely threaten our viability. It had to do with risk adjustment. Risk adjustment was one of the so-called three Rs of the Affordable Care Act (the other two being risk corridor and reinsurance), which were intended to work in concert to limit market volatility in the first few years of the ACA. As proposed by the Congress, risk adjustment was specifically envisioned to ensure that carriers that enrolled healthier-than-average customers would pay into an industry pool within their respective states. The money then would be channeled directly to competitors that enrolled higher-risk members, evening out the companies' costs and reducing the incentive to avoid potentially costly patients. All insurers in a given state were lumped together—from the small CO-OPs to the large Blue Cross / Blue Shield and United Health Care.

The relative health of a particular carrier's population was obtained thusly: every enrollee of a given insurance company got a score based on how many diagnosis codes they had in their medical records in that calendar year. The sicker they were, the more codes they had, and the higher their score. The scores of all enrollees of each company were added up and an average score generated. The company with the highest average score (and, purportedly, the sickest population) would receive payments directly from the carriers in their state with healthier populations. In theory, this process makes some sense, as it would discourage insurers from advertising only to healthier populations and, therefore, less-expensive enrollees. Thus, it was extremely important to maximize the number of codes you could find in your enrollees' medical records.

The actual technical mechanism of how codes were submitted to CMS is far too complicated to explain here. Suffice it to say that each of the more than 750 insurance companies in the country was to upload its data by April 1, 2015, for its members during the previous year, 2014. This data was submitted to the receptacle for all data—the federal Edge Server at CMS—where extremely complicated formulae generated the final score for each carrier, which determined who paid and who owed what in each state.

In our case, not surprisingly, our TPA was having serious problems getting the Edge Server to accept its data, which delayed some of our early submissions, which were supposed to be submitted as they were obtained by each carrier's TPA. However, due to the troubles of our TPA, we never got preliminary information on how many diagnosis codes were captured from our patients' records; all we knew was that by the skin of their teeth, Care Solutions successfully loaded 98% of our patients' records by April 1.

Breathing a collective sigh of relief, we waited to hear our average risk score, expecting to be owed a modest amount, since we had likely taken on sicker members than CareFirst and would like to have leveled the playing field a bit. (We had formed this opinion because brokers told us they were initially less likely to place their best—read healthiest—groups with an unknown insurer like Evergreen, leaving us with sicker groups and individuals.)

Analyzing this data turned out to be harder than expected for CMS, so the disclosure of the scores dragged on and on. We waited with the rest of the insurers until late summer, when a contact within CMS called us to let us know that there was a serious problem with our data: not even one of our thousands of enrollees had more than a single diagnosis code. We were flabbergasted—that was simply not possible. We knew, for example, that we had dozens of diabetic patients with end-stage kidney disease, high blood pressure, and congestive heart failure—dozens of members with at least four diagnosis codes each. We knew of many more complicated patients, some of whom should have had upward of ten diagnosis codes each. How could we not have more than a single diagnosis code on any of our members?

Our attention now turned to Care Solutions. We quizzed them on what had happened; they constantly denied any plausible explanation. Eventually, a Care Solutions IT staffer unintentionally gave his superiors the explanation on one of the many conference calls between the TPA executives and our executive team: Care Solutions staff had decided on their own that it was too hard to submit all the data in an appropriate fashion with the appropriate codes, so they had decided single-handedly to *strip all but one* of the diagnosis codes on each of our members. Such a critically damaging decision could not have even been imagined.

Stunned by the seriousness of our situation, I called Kevin Counihan, the director of the agency at CMS responsible for oversight of the CO-OPs, to see if an extension or waiver was available. Although sympathetic to our plight and acknowledging that it was not our fault (other than choosing an inept TPA), he informed me that there was no other recourse than assigning us a default charge—a penalty reserved for those very few carriers who hadn't submitted their risk scores correctly. The default charge of a $2.5 million payment (which amounted to close to 20% of our $13 million in premium revenue) was very distressing, since we had originally assumed that we would be receiving a risk adjustment payment rather than being assessed one.

Thus, to quickly generate more revenue to offset our risk adjustment charge, we turned to our sales team. It would be responsible for working with the broker community to sell our policies on the group market (initially to small businesses with fewer than fifty employees, and eventually to large businesses with more than fifty employees). The health insurance broker is a middleman, working either for a brokerage firm or a so-called general agent (a large brokerage that also does billing and other administrative processes for the brokers selling under their auspices). However, unlike most sales positions, in which the salesman is employed by one company and gets commissions based on sales of that company's products or services, insurance carriers do not employ the majority of health insurance brokers. Rather, most brokers are independent proprietors and sell all insurers' policies, ostensibly working in the best interest of their client—the business that has contracted with them to obtain the best benefit plan for their employees at the best cost.

Unfortunately, the varying commissions paid by different carriers in a market provide an incentive to sell a potentially inferior product to a client. This often means a "war of commissions" between competing carriers—when one raises their commission, the others follow suit or lose customers. In 2016 CareFirst, perturbed that they were losing small businesses to Kaiser and Evergreen, implemented a special bonus (on top of the normal commission) that rewarded brokers for bringing business back to CareFirst from a competitor. Not surprisingly, their share of the small group business started rising as soon as the bonus was announced.

Although the commissions paid by the different carriers were very important to brokers, it wasn't all that mattered to them. They also cared about how responsive an insurance company was to them and their clients. Here, Evergreen clearly outperformed the big companies. We prided ourselves on our customer service to our brokers. I gave my cell phone number to all brokers, so they could get to the head of Evergreen with a request, like adding a member they had accidentally left off of an enrollment form (which otherwise would have precluded that individual from obtaining insurance until the next year's enrollment period). They could also reach our chief medical officer, Dr. Barry Lewis, to get a colonoscopy approved for payment for a 40-year-old woman with a family history suggestive of a need for this screening test (when her previous insurance company refused to pay for a colonoscopy until she turned 50, as strict guidelines recommended). In addition, I always made myself available when our sales reps, Pam Cochran, Chrissy Sobotka, or Kim Connelly, had a meeting with a broker and a potential major client to assure the company's executive staff that we personally cared about their business.

This personal connection wasn't always determinative of a successful sale, but it was an example of how differently a CO-OP could operate compared to the legacy health insurers, who would otherwise completely control the marketplace.

In addition to providing responsive broker services, we also worked very hard to give personalized service to our individual clients. The entire staff at Evergreen was inculcated with the need to put patients first from the time of their orientation, but one of those who could always be counted on to go the extra mile to put this philosophy into practice was John Wolf. Just one of the myriad examples of John's efforts to make things work for our patients is highlighted in the following letter from the sister of one of our insured clients:

> The delay in sending this email in no way negates my gratitude for everything you did to help my brother during his recent health crisis. After nearly two weeks of facing one obstacle after another in getting his prescription(s) filled for his diabetes, and not being able to get any assistance from his primary care doctor, who he found out at the time wasn't in the Evergreen network he is enrolled in, I was relieved to reach you on November 4th.
>
> As I mentioned on the phone, my brother has a number of chronic conditions for which daily medication is critically important, and for which a lapse in medication could have had a catastrophic effect. Our mom passed away from uncontrolled diabetes, so not being able to get his diabetes medication increased my brother's anxiety . . . From the minute you answered my call, you sprang into action by not only getting to the cause of the issue that was preventing his prescription from going through the system, but you referred me to your Rotunda office in hopes of being able to get him an appointment with a doctor who could get him the medical attention he was desperately in need of. I immediately called . . . and was fortunate to speak with Kathleen, who, like you, understood the magnitude of his issue(s) and got him in to see a doctor that afternoon. You then called me back shortly thereafter to advise that his prescription/pharmacy issue had been resolved, allowing him to get his much-needed medication.
>
> Thank you doesn't seem like nearly enough for all you did to help us during our time of crisis.

Again, this level of personalized service was a defining attribute of many of the CO-OPs and highlighted the benefits they could provide in the states in which they existed.

Unfortunately, however, a significant impediment to the future success of

CO-OPs was the virtual prohibition on their acquiring capital from third parties, a remnant of the fiscal cliff negotiations back at the end of 2012. This was a crucial obstacle because of the requirement to maintain an arbitrarily high level of reserves at 500% risk-based capital, despite state regulations requiring only a 200% RBC level for other insurers in Maryland and elsewhere. As the CO-OPs captured larger enrollment, they needed additional solvency dollars to continue to meet the 500% RBC level. However, CMS had no additional funds to assist with the solvency needs of the growing CO-OPs.

Despite this lack of capital, about a dozen CO-OPs had significant enrollments (in the range of 40,000 to 200,000 members—Evergreen had about 20,000) by mid-2015. However, significant chinks in their financial armor were coming into view, and by October, over half of the CO-OPs had failed and closed shop. Ironically, the majority of the CO-OPs that went down were the very same high enrollers that had threatened to take over Evergreen just a year earlier. What had happened to them in the interim?

The largest CO-OPs gained their large enrollments predominantly by underpricing their competitors on their state or federal exchanges—a practice strongly supported by CMS. In fact, CMS conducted seminars for CO-OPs on how to price to buy market share with protections of the ACA's three Rs (risk adjustment; risk corridor; and reinsurance). Several CO-OPs bought the argument and decided they should go after a sizeable share of their state's individual market, often by offering significantly lower premiums than their competitors.

By having the lowest or close to lowest premiums, these CO-OPs obtained significant shares of the individual exchange enrollment in their respective states. This meant that they likely signed up a relatively less healthy population than average because a sizeable percentage of these enrollees had not been previously insured and often had pent-up demands based on untreated or undertreated conditions. Some were even sicker, as their preexisting condition (for example, severe diabetes or cancer) may have previously made them uninsurable, a practice now banned by the ACA. With these relatively high-risk members, the high-enrollment CO-OPs burned through their cash to pay the higher than average number of claims. This put them in a tenuous financial position, but they all relied on the backstop of the three Rs, which had been put in place to protect insurers from excessive losses if they enrolled too many customers with expensive medical conditions, to come to the rescue.

Seeing that they had taken on a seemingly sicker population than average, the CO-OPs universally expected to be recipients of risk adjustment payments from their intrastate competitors with healthier populations. The large CO-OPs in New York and Kentucky expected over $100 million in such payments. However, as it turned out, new entrants into the marketplace were severely disadvantaged by the risk adjustment process and formula, resulting in all but two of the twenty-three CO-OPs being assessed significant risk adjustment charges rather than receivables—some to the tune of more than 50% of their entire premium revenue!

In fact, the entire risk adjustment formula and process was skewed heavily in favor of large preexisting carriers, resulting in large payments from smaller, quickly growing carriers to the large ones. The reasons for this inequity were fivefold:

1. CO-OPs did not have years of claims experience to help them identify their sickest members; large insurers identified their sicker members from their codes the year before and made every effort to get them to the doctor in the current year to obtain and document their codes.

2. Large insurers had vastly greater administrative capabilities for chasing these healthcare codes so important in the risk adjustment calculations, as well as a twelve-year history with a similar risk adjustment process in Medicare Advantage plans.

3. CO-OPs had no long-term relationship with their provider network and thus had a more difficult time educating those providers on correct coding.

4. The large insurers took advantage of the administration's allowing grandfathering of many existing plans, which tended to have healthy enrollees who were excluded from the risk adjustment calculations; in other words, the large, preexisting insurers appeared to have sicker enrollees than they actually did—resulting in large receivables paid to them by the new small entrants in the marketplace, which had none of these advantages.

5. Pharmacy claims couldn't be used for the risk adjustment score (patients' conditions can often be inferred from a prescription—for example, an individual who takes insulin is a diabetic), but this was inexplicably explicitly not allowed in the methodology.

The CO-OPs with particularly high risk adjustment payouts, and which faced gigantic financial losses, had one potential reprieve. The risk corridor program was supposed to rebate money to insurers that had claims far larger than their premiums could support. Funded by financial "winners" on the exchange, this had the potential to make some of the CO-OPs financially whole. Indeed, most CO-OPs counted on their risk corridor receivables to balance out their risk adjustment payouts. However, eight times more in risk corridor receivables were requested by carriers than the amount paid into the pool. Because a little-known Republican-led amendment to the congressional continuing resolution funding bill at the end of 2014 had prohibited any funds other than those paid into the pool to be used to cover risk corridor payments, CMS could only pay 12.5 cents on the dollar (one-eighth) of the $2.87 billion in insurer requests for risk corridor payments. Although they had clearly seen this coming for months, CMS didn't tip off the industry until one month before open enrollment, on October 1, 2015, when it announced this risk corridor funding shortage.

After CO-OPs learned that they would receive only a small fraction of their requested risk corridor payment, leaving most financially strapped with huge losses, all but eleven of the twenty-three closed their doors by December 2015.

Chapter Five

Improving Fortune

November 2015 to March 2016

Following the failure of more than half of the original twenty-three CO-OPs, representing more than $1 billion in lost taxpayer dollars, Congress suddenly took notice. Never expressing much interest in how well the CO-OP program had been run during its launch and implementation, the Republican-controlled Senate and House of Representatives smelled blood. With their fifty-plus votes to abolish the Affordable Care Act (a.k.a. Obamacare) producing no tangible results, and with the potential that the ACA would fall off the radar screen as a major issue in the upcoming 2016 national election, the heavily publicized failures of the CO-OPs gave the GOP a new stick with which to attack the ACA and refocus attention on its problems.

Indeed, starting in November 2015, five separate committees of the US Congress held hearings on the CO-OP program. First came a subcommittee hearing on November 3, of the House Ways and Means Committee, in which Dr. Mandy Cohen, the chief of staff to the Centers for Medicare and Medicaid Services administrator Andy Slavitt, was the main witness. Two days later, a subcommittee hearing of the House Energy and Commerce Committee was held, and I was called to testify. I was joined by the insurance commissioners of Louisiana and Tennessee (both states with failed CO-OPs) and by John

Morrison, a former insurance commissioner of Montana, who had played a large role nationally in the development of the CO-OP program.

In my opening statement, I made the following major points:

1. Many of the continued challenges that CO-OPs face could be remedied with simple changes in rules promulgated by CMS, the administration's own agency tasked with implementing the ACA.

2. None of the changes would require an act of Congress or any legislative changes. For example, raising outside capital would allow CO-OPs to use these funds to increase market share and hire staff; this policy change would simply require a CMS rule change.

3. The greatest ongoing financial challenge to CO-OPs was the risk adjustment program. CMS should heed the recommendations as laid out in a letter to Health and Human Services secretary Sylvia Burwell: exempt new and fast-growing plans from risk adjustment for the first three to five years and place a cap on the amount of a plan's risk adjustment transfer charge as a percentage of premium revenue.

Having raised these points, particularly having noted that no legislation need be passed (a bipartisan vote in favor of any change in the ACA was basically a nonstarter), one would expect some questions regarding the veracity of that claim and whether the changes I was advocating would make a real difference for the surviving CO-OPs. However, I knew better, because as often happens with congressional hearings, the witnesses are just window dressing for the legislators to make their points.

Despite promises (on the part of the GOP majority) to further investigate why so many CO-OPs failed and (on the part of the Democrats) to encourage CMS to make some of the changes in its purview to help the remaining CO-OPs survive, nothing happened.

In January 2016, the Senate weighed in, with a hearing of the powerful Finance Committee, where CMS administrator Andy Slavitt testified. Our Senate champion, Ben Cardin, was on the committee. I worked with Dr. Beth Vrabel, his lead health staffer, on briefing materials. Since Cardin was one of the senators most knowledgeable about the details of the ACA, we provided him with specific information on how risk adjustment was affecting small new insurers in general, and CO-OPs in particular.

We gave him information on our innovative value-based insurance design diabetes product, which removed all financial barriers to care that had been shown to stem or even reverse the progression of diabetes, resulting in healthier patients and lower costs due to avoided consequences of untreated diabetes. Ironically, such an innovative approach resulted in more money being owed for risk adjustment payments: it reduced the number and severity of diagnosis codes because it produced better health outcomes than for members of insurance plans that didn't provide these benefits. In making our point that this was one of the unintended consequences of the flawed risk adjustment formula, Senator Cardin put Slavitt on the spot by forcing him to acknowledge the benefits of having CO-OPs like Evergreen. After learning about Evergreen's innovative insurance/PCO model and the devastating effect a large risk adjustment payment would have on Evergreen, Slavitt complimented Evergreen in his testimony on its successes: "Evergreen, from what I know, is exactly the kind of example of the kind of competition and innovation you need from small companies that was envisioned in the CO-OP legislation." Later, after Cardin suggested that Slavitt place a cap on risk adjustment payments of no more than 2% of a carrier's premium revenue, Slavitt said, "We are looking forward to supporting Evergreen as it continues its growth."

Again, however, not much seemed to have been accomplished in pushing for CMS to temporarily change the risk adjustment process by capping payments for three years until major changes were scheduled. But this lack of action on any front didn't keep more hearings from being called. At the end of February, a subcommittee of the House Government Oversight Committee again grilled Mandy Cohen of CMS, and in early March a subcommittee of Senate Homeland Security and Foreign Affairs took up the topic.

Having seemingly milked as much political capital out of the failed CO-OPs as possible, congressional interest in the program retreated to its previous low level at the end of early 2016. Despite the failure of more than half of the CO-OPs by the end of 2015, it was clear that most of them had improved competition in their markets. A study of premiums in all states showed that states with a CO-OP had premiums that were 7%–9% lower than those in states without a CO-OP in their market. In addition, CO-OPs had been on the cutting edge of moving from paying for volume to paying for value. For example, of the eleven CO-OPs that remained, three had implemented value-based insurance design programs, including Evergreen's diabetes support program.

What could be done to improve the chances of the remaining CO-OPs surviving and eventually thriving? The same things we had laid out to Slavitt after our initial meeting with him in November of 2015. The two largest obstacles to the CO-OPs' survival in 2016 were the inability to raise additional capital to allow enrollment to grow and, most critically, the negative effect of the risk adjustment formula on CO-OPs and other new small insurers.

Thanks in part to CareFirst being granted a 30% increase in premiums for the individual exchange market, we almost tripled the number of enrollees from the exchange in the third open enrollment period (November 1, 2015, to January 31, 2016) compared to the previous year. With these 11,500 individuals added to our 24,000 members from small groups and 3,000 from large groups (employers with more than 50 employees), we finished the first quarter of 2016 with approximately 38,500 members—more than twice the number of enrollees during the previous year.

Combined with tight financial management and a focus on wellness, primary care, and care-coordination efforts, we started turning a profit. We ended the first quarter of 2016 with profits each month, for a cumulative positive return of over half a million dollars. With all signs pointing to a profitable year—which would set us up to be able to start repaying our loan in 2017—the only thing standing in the way of true success remained the looming threat of risk adjustment.

To address the risk adjustment issue, two other CO-OP CEOs and I got a meeting with CMS director Andy Slavitt in early January 2016. As I pointed out in that meeting, Evergreen was poised to post a very modest loss of $3 million (on $80 million in revenue) for all of 2015 and had even turned a profit each month of the third quarter. However, this loss would rapidly balloon if the risk adjustment formula continued to apply to us and other small carriers in its current form. To avoid catastrophic risk adjustment payables, which would seriously threaten the survivability of the remaining eleven CO-OPs, a temporary reprieve was necessary.

We proposed a simple temporizing option: a "circuit breaker," capping the assessed risk adjustment payable by a new nonprofit insurer at no more than 2% of premium revenue for the year. Despite acknowledging that the risk adjustment process was inequitable—an acknowledgment made tacit by CMS's plan to have a nationwide forum in March 2016 on changing the risk adjustment process, Slavitt refused to provide temporary relief to the new small entrants—including CO-OPs—who were so adversely affected. He added that whatever recommendations came out of the forum would not be implemented until 2018.

Why was CMS so adamant about refusing to temporarily amend risk adjustment? In the course on public policy I taught at Johns Hopkins University, I always told my students that if some policy decision doesn't make sense on the surface, either follow the money or follow the power (the former often strengthens the latter).

The only opposition to the temporary solution we were advocating would come from the big insurers, who would lose a small portion of the money they were to receive under the current flawed formula, and who were all part of a massive political action organization and were major contributors to congressional campaigns. But a look at the actual financial impact of these receivables shows that the loss to large insurers was *miniscule* compared to the impact of the risk adjustment payables to the CO-OPs, as the following example from Maryland highlights:

- Evergreen's original estimated $10 million payable for 2015 was 12% of Evergreen's 2015 premiums of $80 million (the final assessment would change dramatically in short order).
- That same $10 million receivable for CareFirst was 0.2% of Care First's $4.6 billion in premiums (2014 data).

One can only conclude that CMS was facilitating a much more meaningful consequence for large insurers: eliminating many of the new competitors in the various state markets. This would occur because the large risk adjustment amounts severely affected the viability of many of the new small entrants (including CO-OPs). However, the impact went far beyond these new insurance carriers. Not addressing the consequences of keeping the current risk adjustment formula and process was the single biggest threat to one of the Affordable Care Act's primary goals. By knocking many of the new entrants out of their respective markets, CMS would be complicit in reducing the affordability of health coverage in those markets. As premiums continued to rise, young and healthy individuals would be priced out of the market. As they left, premiums would continue to rise to cover the costs of expensive, sick patients. The so-called death spiral would develop in affected markets, effectively destroying the ACA.

Even for those insurance carriers that survived, rates would be much higher in the future, not because of poor health outcomes, but because of the uncertainty related to how much and who would be paying out risk adjustment payments in a given market. That was because the rates for the upcoming policy year had to be filed with their respective state's insurance department before the results from risk adjustment for *two years prior* were known. Carriers had in effect to make an estimate for two years hence of the results of a program that had generated very volatile results. The only prudent thing for carriers to do in the face of such uncertainty was to make the next year's premiums dramatically higher.

Both of the above scenarios came to pass within the next couple of years.

In late April 2016, Manny Sheldon, our CFO, popped his head into my office and asked me to come over to see him. Thinking he would confirm that we had just completed the third straight month of the new year with a profit, my heart sank when he told me to close the door. "We just got the estimate for our risk adjustment payment from Milliman (our actuaries)—are you ready? TWENTY-TWO MILLION!" Shocked by the magnitude of the number, I sat stunned: that was more than 27% of our entire premium revenue, which would go straight to our chief competitor's bottom line—because of the risk adjustment formula that CMS had refused to fix.

Even worse, Manny pointed out, was that we only had a little over $27 million in reserves, which would leave us with only $5 million or so after the risk adjustment payout; far below the reserve level required by the state to operate. To protect our members from personally being on the hook for claims that surpassed our reserves, the Maryland Insurance Administration would have to shut us down—likely within months—if we had to pay the full risk adjustment charge. Once again, we were fighting for our lives (for both the CO-OP and the PCOs) and for the health security of our 40,000 CO-OP members.

For several months, I had been talking to the new Maryland insurance commissioner, Al Redmer, about a possible state-based solution to the looming risk adjustment payment (although we had no idea at the time that it would be so large). A former state legislator, who then served as the insurance commissioner for Republican governor Robert Ehrlich in the early 2000s, Redmer had just started his second stint as commissioner, this time under the administration of Gov. Larry Hogan, the surprise victor in Maryland's 2014 gubernatorial race. A rare moderate Republican in these politically polarized times, Redmer had been very supportive of Evergreen—far more so than the Democratic administration of my former boss, Martin O'Malley. Truly believing in the free market, Redmer bristled at CareFirst's monopolistic presence and seemed very pleased that Evergreen was injecting a refreshing degree of competition into what had been a stagnant market.

The commissioner's staff bent over backward to ensure that the forms we filed outlining our proposed insurance policies were responded to quickly. In a show of support, Redmer was so incensed with the behavior of Care Solutions that he launched a market conduct examination of them, the first time a third-party administrator had been audited in anyone's memory.

Having thus far run into a brick wall on risk adjustment, I proposed to the commissioner that he consider issuing an order, imposing the 2% cap we had proposed to CMS, but only on carriers in his jurisdiction.

Intrigued, he asked his staff to look into the legality of such an order, because federal law generally supersedes state law. Although the Maryland attorney general's office cast doubt on the legitimacy of such an action, we retained Covington and Burling, a well-respected law firm in Washington, DC, known for addressing federal-state conflicts. They thought Redmer had some legal ground to stand on, postulating that the federal requirement to transfer funds from one insurer to another without the state's acquiescence could be viewed as an unconstitutionally imposed tax on carriers within a state, whose sole regulator was the state insurance administration, not the federal government. Additionally, state law could reasonably be read as giving the insurance commissioner the power to issue orders to stabilize the marketplace for consumers; keeping the risk adjustment process unchanged would do the opposite. Using this information, we actually wrote a draft order for our insurance commissioner, imposing a cap on insurers' risk adjustment assessments.

Whether or not Redmer could win a legal battle with CMS in court, I urged him to issue the order and force CMS's hand. Either CMS would quietly let the state do what it wanted, saving face by saying that the state, not CMS, regulated its insurers; or CMS could try to force us to pay an exorbitant sum to our competitor, threatening our very survival. CMS would then face the terrible political optics of fighting with a Republican state administration trying to prevent its Obamacare-related CO-OP from being eaten alive by its parent.

Unfortunately, the latter situation would be the one to develop.

PART II / Fighting the Good Fight

Chapter Six

Evergreen Fights Back

April to June 2016

On April 20, 2016, our executive leadership team met with Maryland Insurance commissioner Al Redmer at his office in downtown Baltimore to let him know the magnitude of our estimated risk adjustment payment, and how devastating it would be to our financial state. We pointed out to him that, but for the risk adjustment payments, we would likely turn a profit in only the third year of our existence, ensuring that we would be a real competitor in the marketplace for years to come. We advocated for his issuing the commissioner's order to cap risk adjustment payments now, rather than waiting for the official payment to be assessed by CMS at the end of June. We recommended this timing because it would allow him to express discomfort at the wildly ranging estimates that were floating around (Milliman had originally estimated our payment in a range of $4 to $12 million, with $8 million the most likely—instead of the eventual assessment, which was significantly greater than the worst-case estimate). For the stability of the market and future premium rates, his order would provide assurance to all carriers of who was getting what, and why.

Working against the clock, we set about to garner as much support for the commissioner as we could. I put together a briefing memo for our entire congressional delegation on the flaws of the risk adjustment formula and process, and the fatal effect our payment would represent if unabated. I also laid out the "ask" of our legislators: put pressure on CMS/HHS to accept the commissioner's order without pushback. After calling both of our US senators' chiefs of staff, I was pleasantly surprised to hear that both Senator Barbara Mikulski and Senator Ben Cardin would be meeting with Health and Human Services secretary Sylvia Burwell early the next week. Both senators raised the subject with the secretary; I was informed by staffers who were at the Burwell meeting that she told them that she "thought the problem had been resolved." Assuring her that this was not the case, they both followed up with strong letters to the HHS secretary, requesting that she intervene with CMS.

About this time, I started detailing our travails to my parents. Since I was always very close to both of them, my daily calls with them on my way home from Evergreen took on an important role in my work life. Although my dad had been retired from Congress for almost two decades, my parents had maintained a strong interest in national politics. These calls, in which they provided me with support and advice, not only brought them even closer to me but also seemed to bring them back a hint of their old life. (It also marked somewhat of a return to my adolescent years, when I worked in my dad's California state senate office; our rides home were full of discussions of what was going on in the state capitol building in Sacramento.)

One matter I talked with them about was my call to Matt Lynch, a senior official at CMS (who often made clear that he didn't have much decision-making power), with whom I'd had a good relationship and who was generally a straight shooter. In the call, I strongly laid out the potentially disastrous consequences of risk adjustment for many of the new insurance carriers in the country, as I had been doing ad nauseam for months. He agreed with the general concept, saying that CMS had recently realized that many carriers were likely to be assessed risk adjustment payments of a magnitude similar to ours. He then informed me that CMS was coming out with a new rule (the federal equivalent of a binding regulation of a particular program) later that day that would help a bit in terms of the CO-OPs raising additional capital. When I got the executive summary of the new rule later that afternoon, I was surprised to see how minor the changes were. It didn't seem to me that the new guidelines would be game-changing in the realm of raising capital, particularly since few investors would be interested in a CO-OP faced with the current risk adjustment assessments.

However, upon reading the actual document, I was favorably surprised to read an excerpt from the rule, buried in the last two pages of the document: "We believe that a robust risk adjustment program that addresses new market dynamics due to rating reforms and guaranteed issue is critical to the proper functioning of these new markets. However, we are sympathetic to these concerns and recognize that States are the primary regulators of their insurance markets. *We encourage States to examine whether any local approaches, under State legal authority, are warranted to help ease this transition to new health insurance markets*" (emphasis mine).

Following the release of the new rule, apparently giving significant leeway to the states to address the risk adjustment flaws themselves, Redmer went to Washington to meet with the higher-ups in CMS. He laid out a few options that CMS would reasonably be expected to approve, considering their recent guidance on the states' authority to deal with risk adjustment: a cap of a few different percentages of a specific carrier's premium revenue, or a post-assessment redistribution of the payment within Maryland to achieve the same goal as a cap. Redmer reported back that Kevin Counihan, the number two official at CMS, had been relatively sympathetic to his entreaties that the state should manage its own risk adjustment transfers, though he had not confirmed that CMS would acquiesce.

During a meeting at the Maryland Insurance Administration in mid-May, Redmer informed me of an idea he had about remediating the risk adjustment transfers within Maryland—a proposal he had floated with Chet Burrell, the CEO of CareFirst: "either Evergreen's risk adjustment payment of an estimated $22 million stands and they go out of business, netting CareFirst zero dollars; or CareFirst goes along with my redistribution plan or cap, which reduces Evergreen's payment to a survivable number, and gets about $6 million now and will be paid the remainder when Evergreen is more flush with funds." Faced with this sensible argument, Burrell reportedly gave Commissioner Redmer a tentative thumbs-up.

A few days later, I got a disconcerting email from Redmer. Despite CMS's rule change, which supposedly gave significant leeway to the state insurance regulators to address the flawed risk adjustment processes in their own states, Redmer told me that he didn't feel he had made any progress with CMS on this issue. They continued to tell him that he could only modify the risk adjustment process *after* we had written a check to CMS for the full estimated $22 million. And, he pointed out, we didn't have the money to write that check. CMS certainly didn't seem to be offering the free rein to the states that they had promised.

Furious that CMS still didn't understand how important this was, and particularly because CMS's stance was going to torpedo the one promising solution for the remaining viable CO-OPs to survive, I sent off a strong email to Lynch at CMS basically saying, What are you thinking?! He promised me that he would meet with the risk adjustment committee at CMS on Monday morning and get back to me on their thoughts on state-based approaches.

Now taking the case to Counihan, Lynch's boss, I laid out the arguments for a temporary cap on risk adjustment payments, especially seeing as the feds would not allow a pre-assessment action by the states, and states seemed not to be able to force post-assessment payments. He was completely intransigent regarding any federal remedy on risk adjustment. I kept saying that they were killing the most viable, profitable CO-OP, and he kept saying "I know," but he argued that the Affordable Care Act was like a balloon: you squeeze one area and it affects something else.

I challenged him, asking what terrible result would occur if a temporary cap were placed on risk adjustment. He said that some carriers had counted on risk adjustment receivables in calculating their premium rates, and those rates would be potentially invalidated should a change be made in risk adjustment. I countered that a $22 million risk adjustment payment was 27% of our premiums, but it was less than 0.3% of CareFirst's premiums, so I seriously doubted it would affect their rates at all. He agreed, and said that was why the CareFirst board should not mind foregoing the $22 million for a sure $6 million or so. After we concluded the call, once again I felt like Alice going through the looking-glass.

As I arrived home that evening, I was beginning to think that we might have gone through our nine lives and that things simply weren't going to work out. But Chris reassured me that we were fighting the good fight—we, along with a few other CO-OPs, were doing everything we could to keep true to the ACA's principles of increasing access to affordable high-quality care. Bolstered by her assurances, I returned to work the next day ready to continue to fight to get this huge risk adjustment albatross off our neck before it felled us.

That day, Lynch informed me that he had conferred with the CMS risk adjustment team, and they confirmed that the process had to go forward as planned. While it was true that the new rule released by CMS gave flexibility to the states on how they handled risk adjustment in their own jurisdiction, it would have to occur *after* the CMS transfer process.

So, after proposing no fewer than nine potential solutions to the terribly flawed risk adjustment process, after almost a year of dialogue with officials at the highest levels of the administration, and after all of the efforts of CO-OPs and other new insurers in the same boat with risk adjustment, it came down to this short conversation with Matt Lynch, indicating that CMS didn't seem to care about encouraging new entrants to bring innovation and increased competition to the health insurance markets around the country. Rather, CMS seemed to be confirming that it was firmly in the lap of the big insurance companies, which had controlled the industry for decades. As a big supporter of President Obama and as a lifelong liberal, I had never felt so disillusioned with government as I did that day.

As I wrote later that day to the chair of the Energy and Commerce Committee of the US House of Representatives in response to his questions about CMS's actions regarding risk adjustment: "The bottom line is that by refusing to amend an admittedly defective process of Risk Adjustment, CMS is knowingly causing virtually all of the remaining CO-OPs to fail, costing taxpayers over two billion dollars in loans which will not be repaid. Surprisingly, CMS's inaction is even threatening our CO-OP, which has turned a profit in the 3rd quarter of 2015 and in each of the first four months of this year."

In late May, on one of our frequent calls, Redmer reported on his eagerly anticipated meeting with the board of directors of CareFirst regarding his cap proposal. Everyone's assumption was that CareFirst's self-imposed cap would pass muster with CMS. He informed me that the board was fairly positive about the idea, but had some questions, the most substantive being: Would Evergreen be in the same risk adjustment situation next year? The commissioner assured them that we would not have anything near the magnitude of this payment next year—which was true. We would have a more stable longstanding population of members on whom we had good data (for example, codes), and without a doubt (or so we hoped) the administration of the new president who would be taking office in January 2017—whom we all assumed would be Hillary Clinton—would make changes to the dysfunctional components of the ACA.

Redmer was inclined to give CareFirst a couple of weeks to decide. I reminded him that our drop-dead date was June 30, when the risk adjustment payments would be officially assessed—and the date on which our reserves would fall to an unacceptable level. I asked that he get their answer by the next week so that we could pursue other options if CareFirst turned us down.

Our champion, the Republican insurance commissioner, went to bat for us that afternoon against CMS for one last try at getting them to consider any type of cap or other temporary solution at the federal level. He called me on his car ride back from CMS, telling me he had never had a meeting as frustrating as that one. Not only did they not budge, but he was also irked by their utter lack of interest in resolving the situation that would kill off their own investments, putting thousands of CO-OP employees out of work, causing significant stress to hundreds of thousands of their customers, and assuring that $2.4 billion in loans to the CO-OPs would never be repaid to the taxpayers.

The day ended with Manny, Mary Porter, our legal counsel, and I presenting our situation to the executive committee of the Evergreen board over dinner in Little Italy. Consisting of two original members of the board—Chair Fran Phillips and Vice Chair John Pearson—along with the treasurer, Carolyn Walker, the committee expressed total support for our efforts and vowed to help with the fight.

Meanwhile, to prepare for the worst, I asked Porter to call Covington and Burling, our Washington law firm specializing in regulatory law, to set up a discussion on the merits of filing a case against the federal government. Specifically, we were initially interested in a preliminary injunction (PI) against CMS. If successful, the action would prevent us from being assessed a risk adjustment payment by CMS, at least until the actual case had been decided.

On May 26, during our board meeting, a few of us adjourned to a small conference room for a call to our outside attorneys at Covington and Burling to hear their thoughts on the viability of filing for the injunction. They were optimistic on our chances of prevailing against CMS—they felt that we should be able to overcome the threshold of proving there would be irreparable harm should the injunction not be granted (since the current risk adjustment payment would put us out of business). More encouraging, the lawyers felt we could actually win the overall case, using two lines of reasoning: capricious and arbitrary administrative actions; and illegal lack of payment of risk corridor.

Not wanting to blindside Commissioner Redmer, who was pursuing the loan from CareFirst (which would get nothing from us if we were successful with the suit), I called him to say that we were preparing for such action but would not move forward unless he'd heard nothing positive by the following week. Appreciative of the heads-up, he said he understood completely.

Later in the day I blasted CMS and HHS for their callousness and obstinacy to two reporters—one from Bloomberg *News* and one, Paul Demko, a friendly and very knowledgeable reporter for *Politico*. While this allowed me to vent some steam, it wasn't without strategic purpose—I wanted to proactively bring the indefensible position of CMS to the fore publicly, in order to get support from other quarters.

Knowing that we had a reasonable chance to win our lawsuit, I realized that if we won, every insurer in the country who would be hurt by risk adjustment payments would likely follow suit. If some of them were also successful, this would threaten the viability of the entire ACA, as it would lead to the large insurers mounting a challenge to the risk adjustment changes. Not wanting that to happen, and seeing the potential leverage that created for us, I emailed Jim Messina, President Obama's former deputy chief of staff. I outlined our problems and asked him to pass along a memo detailing the simple solution that could obviate them (a temporary federal cap or waiver for risk adjustment payments) to someone in the White House who could tell the secretary of HHS to just do it. On the memo I included Valerie Jarrett (senior counsel to the president), Denis McDonough (chief of staff), and President Obama.

On Friday, May 27, quiet reigned, although my daughter Jane called to tell me that she'd heard I had "thrown rocks at CMS." She was referring to a quote I gave *Politico*'s Paul Demko:

> CAN RISK ADJUSTMENT BE FIXED?—Earlier this month, HHS announced that it was seeking proposals from state regulators for how to tweak the risk adjustment program to protect insurers. Many smaller and startup health plans have complained that the program has forced them to essentially subsidize their wealthier, better-established counterparts.
>
> Many of the co-ops praised the move as a welcome indication that CMS was listening to their concerns. But those warm feelings have dissipated—to put it mildly, Pro's Paul Demko reports. Peter Beilenson, CEO of Maryland's Evergreen Health, one of four Obamacare startups to turn a profit in the first quarter of this

year, says the state's insurance department has brought at least five proposals to CMS in recent weeks—and every single one has been shot down. He's concluded that the agency has no intention of making substantive changes that would help plans potentially facing big risk adjustment payments.

"They are knowingly causing all of the remaining co-ops to fail, costing taxpayers over a billion dollars," Beilenson tells PULSE. "They're eating their own. It's idiotic; it's imbecilic."

The piece garnered positive feedback from other CO-OP CEOs and supporters, pleased that someone was pulling the curtain open on CMS's actions. In addition, as we hoped, pursuing media coverage did lead to several federal legislators, favorable to the ACA, picking up the torch on the effort to change the risk adjustment formula.

That day, a similar article came out in Bloomberg *BNA's Health Report*. This time my points were also backed up by officials in New Mexico, Massachusetts, and by Redmer himself:

Maryland Insurance Commissioner Redmer, appointed by Gov. Larry Hogan (R), told Bloomberg BNA he has had no success at getting the CMS to approve changes he thinks need to be made to keep Evergreen operating. "I'm looking for any flexibility," he said, "and at this point we have not found any." Redmer said he has met with Mandy Cohen, chief operating officer and chief of staff of the CMS, as well as Kevin Counihan, director of the CMS's Center for Consumer Information and Insurance Oversight and marketplace chief executive officer. "Sadly, other than having dozens of conversations, we really are in a place that was no different from a few months ago," Redmer said.

Also weighing in, in support of our claims, was Rick Foster, chief actuary at CMS for almost twenty years, from 1995 to 2013:

Richard Foster, who was the CMS chief actuary from 1995 until 2013 and is now a consultant with Leavitt Partners working for a group of CO-OPs and provider-sponsored plans, told Bloomberg BNA that new plans are being adversely affected by the risk adjustment program. New plans don't have medical claims data on their enrollees, and services provided during the year in which risk adjustment payments are calculated "might not carry accurate diagnoses with them," Foster said. The CMS risk adjustment formula "depends on diagnoses," he said.

Having taken part in the development of risk adjustment, Foster could be a tremendously valuable potential witness if we ended up seeking an injunction against CMS.

We couldn't have asked for better publicity. CMS officials (Counihan and Cohen) were not available to the reporter to respond.

Over the Memorial Day weekend I thought a lot about our options and came to the conclusion that we should take a calculated risk and go ahead with the lawsuit and the associated PI. After bouncing the pros and cons off my wife and my parents, the choice became clear—it was ridiculous to take out a loan from our competitors; taking on CMS/HHS was the right thing to do. I set up a conference call with our leadership team for the following day with an email giving the rationale for my position:

1. I realize that we can stay alive with $16m in surplus note to CareFirst, but it is still a significant liability.

2. *We will never* get a break from CMS on anything or any proposal we make; I don't trust that they wouldn't renege on a deal with CareFirst even if they do initially approve it.

3. I know we will make *every* effort possible to maximize our Risk Adjustment score the next two years, but I am *not* convinced we can beat CareFirst at code chasing, and we still face the uneven playing field (grandfathering and the like) until the 2018 changes. Therefore, I am very concerned that *we will likely face* a similar situation of owing CareFirst significant risk adjustment transfer payments the next two years as well (though maybe of a lesser magnitude).

4. Most importantly, filing suit to take on these fools is the *just* and *right* thing to do. We all know that the RA process is flawed and antithetical to the intent of the ACA. Someone has to take them on (this case will either force their [CMS's] hand to issue a temporary cap/waiver as a settlement *or* they lose and RA goes out the window, threatening the stability of markets across the country).

5. I know it is a gamble, but based on the fact that we have both elements needed to obtain a PI (proof of irreparable harm and likelihood to win on merits of the case), and our attorneys like our chances, I am willing to take this calculated risk.

6. And, if the PI isn't granted we could return to the $6m pay / $16m loan option.

That Monday, however, our executive leadership team persuaded me to alter my viewpoint somewhat, based on a possible complication if we went forward with the injunction first: absent a decision on the lawsuit, we would probably have to record the $22 million estimated payment as a liability on our financial filing with the MIA—basically reporting that we had run out of money. Thus, even though the team—Sheldon, Porter, and Kreiskott—agreed wholeheartedly that filing suit was the right thing to do, it left us in a precarious position. We adjourned, having determined to pursue the proposed deal with CareFirst; but if they didn't acquiesce, we would go forward with the request for an injunction.

On the last day of May 2016, thirty days until the official risk adjustment assessment was to be released by CMS, we started the workweek by organizing our efforts to get the information and documents that our attorneys from Covington and Burling needed to get the case ready for filing. In our conversation with Caroline Brown and Phil Peisch at noon, we decided to pursue our two options (payment/loan with CareFirst or the PI) at the same time. We could use the pursuit of an injunction as a bargaining tool to get CareFirst to put up the loan; and if the CareFirst option fell through, we would have the injunction ready to go before the risk adjustment assessments came out on June 30.

After our call with the lawyers, I updated Redmer, and pressed him on the need to hear from CareFirst soon. He told me that he had given them until the next day at noon to give him their verdict on the partial payment plus the loan. If he didn't hear from them, he was prepared to call their CEO, Chet Burrell. Now it was time to wait as outside forces, over which we had no control, affected our fate yet again.

I texted Redmer at 12:57 p.m.: he had not heard anything. I texted him again, saying that our attorneys had told us that we had to give them the go or no-go message by June 6 if we wanted to file the injunction in time to affect the risk adjustment assessment at the end of the month. Redmer said he had a call with Burrell scheduled for Friday, June 3.

Meanwhile, I had gotten a reply from Jim Messina. He had forwarded my message to the White House director of political affairs, as well as to another former Obama deputy chief of staff, Nancy-Ann DeParle. DeParle was a major player in healthcare reform, having been one of the key architects of the ACA as the director of the White House Office on Health Reform. In her reply to Messina she validated my points in the memo (no legislation was needed, and it was easy for Secretary Burwell to implement our suggested solutions), but she also said that Burwell and Jacob Lew, director of the Office of Management and Budget, were reluctant to demonstrate any flexibility on this topic, for no apparent reason.

After this unsatisfying response, and since we hadn't made any headway with the Obama administration, despite a multitude of efforts from numerous high-level individuals, we decided to approach the Hillary Clinton campaign. Whatever problems befell the ACA would pose a major obstacle to Clinton's presidential campaign, and Donald Trump would potentially use the failure of a large number of CO-OPs against Clinton, a big supporter of Obamacare.

Thus, I finished the day with an email to Nancy-Ann DeParle to see what she thought, because, not only had she been a big player in the Obama administration, she had also served President Bill Clinton as his administrator of CMS. The next day DeParle politely let me know that she could not be of any help as she had been away from the Obama White House for three years and wasn't connected to any of the major players there—she did not even mention the Clintons. I didn't know her personally so I didn't press the matter, but was disappointed nonetheless.

About that time, a bittersweet moment occurred during a meeting at our headquarters between the staffs of our PCOs and staff from the CO-OP. CO-OP staff were explaining how PCO staff could identify the least expensive medications for their patients using the CO-OP website, and PCO staff were making suggestions to CO-OP staff on how to best encourage patients to come in for visits, thus helping risk adjustment. This interaction served to remind me of the value of the innovative model we had built—aligning an insurance company and a provider system to benefit the care and satisfaction of our patients—while having to contemplate its loss due to the stubbornness of a few high-level bureaucrats.

The day ended with an ominous email from Redmer, saying that, although he hoped for the best in awaiting CareFirst CEO Burell's response, he nonetheless had to start working on what he called plan B: to put us into receivership should CareFirst refuse to accept his proposal. This was the first time Al had implied that Evergreen might not survive the risk adjustment debacle, and it was deeply disconcerting.

I got into the office a little before 8 on June 3. A few minutes later, Manny walked into my office and said he had some bad news. "CareFirst is going to say no."

"How do you know that?"

"Our compliance officer talked to a friend of hers at CMS who told her that CMS had—unbeknownst to us—met with Al Redmer to discuss our situation."

Sure enough, a couple of hours later, I received a text message from Redmer: "Hey Peter—just talked to Chet, it's a no—not interested—Sorry, Al." As soon as we got the message, I sent an email titled "CareFirst said no deal . . . WE ARE SUING CMS!" to our executive leadership team as well as our attorneys, and set up a meeting early in the afternoon to put our legal strategy into action. I also asked our communications team to join us.

First, however, we talked with Redmer to learn where he stood. Still on our side (and even more supportive because of his displeasure with CareFirst), he nonetheless had to lay out his approach. He would support our lawsuit and work with us to try to keep us afloat, but at the same time he'd have to prepare to put us in receivership to protect our members should our risk-based capital (the measure of reserves) fall below 200% due to our huge pending risk adjustment payment. (This is a good time to point out that from this time forward Redmer—bending over backward to preserve an important competitor in his state's insurance market—would continue to reduce the RBC level required to be met by Evergreen as long as he could, even over the objections of many of his staff.)

Receivership was basically a death sentence—an independent oversight group would become the receiver and take over daily operations of the company, generally with the goal of closing it by the end of the year—ensuring that claims continued to be paid and a modicum of customer service persisted until shutdown. Under receivership, whether or not I remained at Evergreen, neither the executive leadership team nor I would be in charge of the company.

Redmer said that nothing would be done until at least June 30, when the risk adjustment assessments came out, and we would have to post them as a liability. But more likely, any action would probably be held off until he saw where we were on August 15, the date on which our risk adjustment payment to CMS (which would be sent immediately to CareFirst) was due. If this occurred, we would have insufficient reserves, and Evergreen would go into receivership. (This is a good time to point out that Redmer would also continue to let deadlines slip going forward, as long as we were on a legitimate path to long-term viability.)

Facing an ominous future, we went into our conference call with Brown and Peisch. In my experience, when you have really competent attorneys, talking to them makes you feel as though you have called in the cavalry—they provide a sense of confidence and solidarity for your cause. That was how I felt while talking to them about our legal options.

Our best option was to file a complaint against CMS/HHS immediately, claiming that the risk adjustment process was wrongfully implemented, and go for a preliminary injunction after the June 30 assessment to prevent any payment on August 15. It was easy to file for a PI, and the standard to obtain one—showing a reasonable cause that irreparable harm would occur prior to the actual case being heard—seemed a decent bet to be met by a description of the dire circumstances we would be in after the risk adjustment assessment came down. We adjourned, agreeing to file the initial claim in United States District Court for the District of Maryland late in the coming week.

Now we turned to our communication strategy—and how we would talk to the press when we announced the suit. We identified two primary audiences, to be addressed with different messages and goals: the first was our members and the citizens of Maryland, who would potentially be affected by the demise of Evergreen. For this group, the message was that we had been trying aggressively to change this unfair, flawed part of the ACA for a year, to protect Evergreen and its constituents and also to protect all consumers in Maryland by maintaining competition in the state. Our goal was to raise awareness of the problem and potentially gather supporters from the general public. To reach this group, we would tailor our message and use local print press—the *Baltimore Sun* and business papers, such as the *Daily Record* and *Baltimore Business Journal*.

The second audience was national policy makers, legislators, and opinion leaders. For this group, the message would be like that for the first, but with more specificity about the reasons the risk adjustment process was so flawed, along with the national consequences of the process remaining unchanged (that is, the certitude of much higher insurance premiums due to loss of competition across the country before the presidential election, and the possibility of a death spiral of insurance rates, should healthy folks be priced out of the market). We would use the major national print and online outlets—the *New York Times, Washington Post, Wall Street Journal,* and *Politico*—to publicize this. We hoped that legislators and thought leaders would be so taken by the inexplicable intransigence of CMS/HHS that pressure would build to get them to change the rules—somewhat of a blue-sky hope, but desperate times called for desperate measures.

That evening while driving my son Jack to a get-together with his friends, our conversation was interrupted by a call from Congressman Elijah Cummings, who had been a longtime supporter of Evergreen and was following the media coverage of the risk adjustment issue. I laid out the frustrations of the past couple of months. Telling me that HHS and CMS clearly knew his and the delegation's displeasure at their actions, he expressed his own irritation with the lack of progress. Getting back to his duties in Detroit, he told me he'd "call Valerie later that evening" (Valerie Jarrett, the closest confidante in the White House to both the president and first lady).

Figuring that much of the Evergreen staff was now starting to hear about the seriousness of the risk adjustment situation, we decided to address the subject in a staff meeting. This was in keeping with our longstanding practice of having all-staff meetings to keep our colleagues up to date on issues related to Evergreen. The topics had included a detailed description of our budget, an annual presentation of new products we would be offering, as well as team-building exercises. In this case, our senior leadership team agreed unanimously that we had to project confidence in our ability to overcome the risk adjustment issue, either by legal action or by securing financing to make the payment. We should also convey our pride that we were now a profitable, well-functioning player in the Maryland market and were taking on the federal government over an unjust system that hurt consumers and new market entrants alike.

The meeting went far better than we thought it would. Our senior executives projected confidence in our eventual success, and the staff seemed genuinely proud that we were fighting so hard for the organization. Several asked if they could write letters or generate support, portraying the company as strong and united in its effort.

The following day, I ran into a CMS project officer who was at Evergreen to participate in yet another CMS-required audit, this time conducted by the consulting firm Deloitte. The project leader from Deloitte opened the meeting by laying out the purpose of the audit: to provide us with practical information that could improve our performance and to let the CO-OP program at CMS know how we were doing. The reality was that everyone from Evergreen and Deloitte knew that the actual purpose of the visit was to ascertain what our financial situation would be after the risk adjustment payment was made, to see if CMS would be shutting down any new enrollment for us, and to be sure that we had enough financial wherewithal to be able to pay our members' claims for the rest of the year.

But I played along. When they asked me for introductory remarks, I told them that their several-months' timeline until the delivery of their findings would be of little relevance to us if risk adjustment wasn't remediated. I then went into my well-honed diatribe on the risk adjustment saga. The CMS representative noted that she would definitely report our dismay with risk adjustment to the higher-ups at CMS. Thanking her, I said that would be tremendously useful. I'm not sure if she caught my sarcasm.

Trouble didn't stop just because we were in an all-day meeting. Checking in with me mid-morning, Al Redmer (whom I was now talking or texting with virtually daily) made it clear that he would put us in receivership on June 30 when the payment was announced if we didn't have enough reserves on hand to cover the payment. This was new information to us—he had previously said he would probably not pull the trigger until the payment had to be made on August 15. I asked Mary Porter to confirm that with the counsel for the MIA, Van Dorsey, but he wasn't available.

With our legal plan in place, though with no guarantees of success, Manny and I started "dialing for dollars"—trying to find an investor, any investor to give us a loan to provide us with enough reserves to survive our soon-to-be-imposed risk adjustment payment. We knew that the risk adjustment charge would cause our reserves to plummet to an untenable level. Indeed, we expected to need loans totaling $10 to $15 million to get to a risk-based capital reserve level acceptable to our regulators at the MIA.

First I tried our foundation partners from the PCO line of credit—but there wasn't much interest initially to guarantee another, bigger loan, even though we were arguably a fairly good risk, being profitable with a potentially strong business outlook. Then I talked to my colleague Tom Policelli, with the Massachusetts CO-OP. He was trying to grease the skids with his board to possibly loan us some of their remaining surplus dollars they had yet to draw down. There were positive vibes from his board, but if they approved it, CMS would have to agree as well, which was not a given.

Next, I called Kevin Counihan, the number two official at CMS, not using my cell. Picking up because my name did not appear on his phone, he was clearly surprised to hear from me, but listened intently as I ran a proposal by him that CMS administrator Andy Slavitt had suggested in one of our meetings earlier in the year. In January, Slavitt told a group of CO-OP CEOs who were worried about risk adjustment that he had made a deal with more than one state insurance department and the CO-OP in that state to have the CO-OP pay a small portion of their assessed payment in that year, and "mortgage" the remaining payment over the next few years. At that time—when we still held out hope for a cap or a waiver—I was adamantly opposed to that idea, as it still had the CO-OP paying an outrageous amount of money, albeit not at once.

Now facing desperate circumstances, I asked Counihan to ask Slavitt to consider the same deal with Evergreen and the MIA. He said he would do that, but he called me a few hours later to inform me, "very bluntly," that I "shouldn't count on it" because another unnamed federal agency had put the kibosh on the process. I didn't even bother to ask why it had been allowed the previous year, because CMS hadn't been helpful or responsive in a timely manner before, and I didn't want to waste any of our precious time pursuing this avenue any further.

My final attempt of the day was a long shot—asking George Soros, the liberal Hungarian-American billionaire (who had encouraged his Open Society Foundation board to guarantee our PCO loan) to guarantee a $10 million loan that we should be able to get from our bank. To get to him, I went through the president of his Baltimore office, Diana Morris, who was warm to the idea and sent along a memo requesting his help. With the possibility of another few million from the Massachusetts CO-OP, we might be able to cobble together enough guarantees to cover a $15 million loan, which would leave us with the reserves we needed to survive.

Meanwhile, Mary Porter had gotten in touch with Commissioner Redmer's legal counsel, Van Dorsey, who provided some useful information. He advised her that discussions were under way at the MIA about what action would be taken, and when, and that the commissioner didn't need to wait until the June financials were closed and RBC calculated, but rather that they were considering action under the Impaired Entities section of Maryland law. "Impaired Entities" sounded scary—and it was, because this portion of the law talked about receivership and closing the company.

Mary told Dorsey that we would provide him with the draft federal complaint and continue discussions with him and the commissioner so that we'd know what they were considering, including the timing of any action. She also said that we would provide him with updates on our efforts regarding the litigation and search for capital.

Matt Jablow, our communications director, came by to talk about how we would message our press coverage when we filed our initial complaint against CMS with the federal court on Monday. If brokers were already skittish just because they knew that risk adjustment would be damaging to us, how would they react when we filed suit? Brokers were the key to maintaining our enrollment during this difficult period. If they got spooked by the legal action, they would probably switch the group business they had placed with us to a more viable competitor—likely CareFirst. Should we say we're pursuing justice for the little guy in a terribly disadvantaged position? What do I say when a reporter asks what will happen if we don't prevail with a preliminary injunction? Realizing that we were in yet another perilous position, this time in the arena of public perception, Jablow retreated to try to develop a message that covered the situation but projected confidence as well—easier said than done.

We decided to send a blast email explaining our rationale for the suit to brokers all over Maryland, while also having our sales staff call all the brokers with whom they worked. This communication effort, along with our reputation for quick personalized service to brokers paid off. For the next several months, brokers expressed their confidence in Evergreen by keeping their groups with us, though not often adding new business.

Midday on June 8, amid breathless proclamations in the media, CMS came out with new rules on risk adjustment:

> Today we are announcing two additional important changes to Risk Adjustment that we intend to propose in future rulemaking. First, we intend to propose that, beginning for the 2017 benefit year, the risk adjustment model include an adjustment factor for partial-year enrollees. Second, we intend to propose that, beginning for the 2018 benefit year, prescription drug utilization data be incorporated in risk adjustment, as a source of information about individuals' health status and the severity of their conditions.

This was good news in that we had succeeded in getting them to pay attention to the flaws of the risk adjustment process. The problem was that the changes didn't take effect for two more years—and Evergreen, along with other small entrants, might not survive that long.

Why did they come out with these new rules now, two years out? When the massive risk adjustment payments were announced at the end of the month, many carriers, insurance commissioners, and consumers would be irate. By putting out the new rules two years early, they hoped to push back on the blame by saying that they had heard the complaints and made changes that would ameliorate at least some of the issues with the risk adjustment formula. Unfortunately, many of the small new insurers, who were detrimentally affected by the current risk adjustment formula, would not be in existence to benefit from these changes when they took effect in 2018.

Unwittingly, CMS's announcement might have given our legal efforts a boost. By explicitly stating that there were ways to more accurately account for actual risk, they were admitting that the current process had not identified actual risk in the ACA plans.

To that end, we had a call with our lawyers and our expert actuarial witness, David Axene, out of California. Just as physician experts are called in a malpractice trial, so would Axene be used in our litigation. It would be his role to discredit CMS's risk adjustment methodology and to show the arbitrary and capricious way in which it was developed, resulting in a flawed estimate of true risk of a carrier's population. After a forty-five-minute conversation, it was clear he knew exactly what he was talking about, and he had two concrete data-driven examples of why our claim that CMS's development of the risk adjustment formula was indeed arbitrary and capricious.

I spent the following Thursday, June 9, in Washington, first with our lawyers, then with our US senator. At the meeting with Caroline Brown and Phil Peisch, Mary Porter and I got the first draft of our complaint. About fifteen pages long, it laid out the facts of the ACA, the risk adjustment methodology, and our allegations that this process was arbitrary and capricious, with evidence to back them up. It concluded with a request to the court to prevent payment of a risk adjustment assessment this year and in future years until the process had been fixed. It was exciting to see the cover page proclaiming: "Evergreen Health Cooperative vs. United States Department of Health and Human Services and Centers for Medicare and Medicaid Services (CMS) and Secretary Sylvia Mathews Burwell and Acting Administrator Andy Slavitt."

Relieved that our efforts to resolve the risk adjustment process of the past ten months were now in print, we discussed the details of the timing of our filing of the complaint for Monday. Porter had finally confirmed with the

MIA's counsel that we had until August 15 to get a successful outcome—either a favorable legal opinion or an adequate loan. Thus, when the risk adjustment assessment came out, on June 30, we would file for a preliminary injunction in United States District Court the following day against the payment due on August 15. The federal government would have two weeks to file its response, then we'd have a week to file our arguments, with affidavits. This would leave plenty of time before August 15 for the judge to either rule directly or call for oral arguments. I left the meeting buoyed by our talk, and ready for David to take on Goliath.

From there I headed to the Hart Senate Office Building to meet with our senator, Ben Cardin, to give him a heads-up on the impending lawsuit. He listened to my description of our efforts to get CMS/HHS to move over the past year and expressed disbelief at their intransigence, saying he would try Secretary Burwell one more time because he couldn't believe that she would allow this to happen if she really knew what was going on. As I left, thanking him for his continued support (as well as that of his chief of staff, Chris Lynch), he noted his approval for the lawsuit, saying that we clearly had to do it.

Most of Friday the tenth was spent revising the lawsuit. Mary, Manny, and I made a few substantive changes to strengthen the complaint and ensure accuracy, and then went back and forth with Brown and Peisch until the document was well-honed. We set two conference calls for the weekend to make the final tweaks in preparation for filing the suit at 1 p.m. on Monday.

The rest of the day was spent preparing for a potential media onslaught and a raft of broker concerns after the complaint had been filed. Matt Jablow called the national reporters who had been covering us for the past few years (Amy Goldstein of the *Washington Post*, Reed Abelson of the *New York Times*, Stephanie Armour of the *Wall Street Journal*, and Paul Demko of *Politico*) to schedule interviews for just after the filing. We went over potential questions and how to handle them. None really concerned me regarding the national media. I was pretty sure we had good answers for why this action was necessary, and a very good explanation of the flaws with risk adjustment. The only thing that still concerned me was how local coverage (the *Baltimore Sun*) would affect the perception of Evergreen by potential customers in Maryland. Would it look as if we were financially sound and were taking on the big bully, fighting for justice? Or would it look as if we were desperate to keep from going under, and this was our only option?

Chapter Seven

Preparing to Go to Court

June 2016

The original lawsuit was filed in federal court in Baltimore at 1:15 p.m., Monday, June 13, and the media requests began shortly thereafter: the *Baltimore Sun*, the *Wall Street Journal*, the *Washington Post*, and the *New York Times*, in rapid succession. Although media was not a part of our legal strategy, since we didn't expect coverage of the case to affect the judge's decision, the fact that the initial articles about the suit were very favorable couldn't hurt in the aftermath of a potential negative decision. The media commentaries focused on the uneven playing field created by risk adjustment, showed us in a position of strength, and gave us credit for taking on the issue for the good of other small entrants. CMS declined to comment for any of the articles, so the messages we pushed went uncontested.

In order to update our partners, shortly after the suit was filed we hosted a webcast for the broker community. Open to all brokers who were interested in learning more about the lawsuit and our situation, the webinar consisted of a brief presentation from me, followed by the submission of questions by the brokers. In general, the twenty or so questions were softballs: most of those listening expressed support for our efforts and congratulations for taking on CMS. There were remarkably few queries about our viability, and no one seemed overly concerned. Of course, the fifty or so brokers on the call may have been those who were already sympathetic, but regardless, their support was appreciated and reassuring.

The most intriguing event of the week was the emergence of a potential whistleblower, when a former CMS employee called us after seeing the press coverage of the lawsuit to tell us that he had some potentially useful information about the development of the risk adjustment formula and methodology.

Although he arrived at CMS after the initial configuration of the risk adjustment methodology had been presented by RTI (the consulting firm given responsibility for creating the formula and methodology), the whistleblower relayed what he called the constant friction between RTI and the leadership of CMS over the problems with the initial methodology. For example, RTI strongly encouraged CMS to include pharmacy data in the formula. CMS opposed, stating there was no need. RTI didn't want the risk adjustment transfers to be a zero-sum game—where there were *winners* and *losers*. Rather, they preferred a system like that used for risk adjustment with Medicare Advantage plans, which attributed more funding to carriers that had sicker members, but did not charge those insurers with healthier populations—a formula that had worked well for a dozen years. He said that CMS disagreed, and kept talking about the need to just get the formula finalized and out to the insurance carriers, paying little attention to the formula's validity.

After talking with him at length, Mary Porter and I were satisfied that his story was plausible, and we turned our informant over to our attorneys to depose him for the upcoming trial—and to get his contacts at RTI to confirm what he had told us. If his account proved true, our case against CMS for arbitrarily and capriciously developing the risk adjustment formula and methodology would be much easier to prove.

Next, I had to prepare my affidavit for the upcoming request for a preliminary injunction, which would be filed in two weeks. My affidavit was the main part of our brief to the judge, so it had to include my background, the history of Evergreen, what made it special, how we were improving the healthcare system, and what would happen to the CO-OP and the PCOs and their staff and members if a preliminary injunction wasn't granted.

A true gift came in the form of a tremendously supportive editorial published in the *Baltimore Sun*. Written by Andy Green, the head of the editorial staff, it clearly explained the complex issue of risk adjustment, declared that we were suing for the right reasons, and presented our arguments lucidly. He made the point strongly that the way the risk adjustment process was working in practice was actually counter to the goals of the ACA—to increase competition in the marketplace and to encourage innovation and increase access to better care at lower cost, as Evergreen was providing. I know you're not supposed to thank editorial writers when they write about you, but this editorial was so well written and explained our position so clearly that I disregarded my own guideline.

Below is an excerpt from the editorial, starting with a great title: "Can Evergreen force Obamacare to live up to its promise?"

> The lawsuit Baltimore's Evergreen Health Cooperative filed this week against the federal government over its implementation of the Affordable Care Act isn't . . . a case of one of the ACA's most eloquent boosters, Evergreen CEO Peter Beilenson, turning against the law, either. Rather, it's a question about whether the ACA actually lives up to its promise to make American healthcare better and more affordable or whether it merely pours more money into a broken system.

We immediately sent a link to the editorial to the foundations considering guaranteeing our loans, as well as to legislators, policy folks, and reporters.

Mary and I also had a conference call with our attorneys, who told us of a sad but fascinating call that they had had with attorneys for a well-respected family-owned insurer in Florida, who had contacted them after reading about our lawsuit. This Floridian insurer, Preferred Medical Plan, had been run by members of the same family for fifty years, and led by Tamara Fox Myerson for the past twenty. As the only female insurance CEO in Florida, she was especially well known, particularly in the Miami-Dade area, where the majority of their 75,000 Obamacare enrollees lived.

Although profitable, when Preferred Medical Plan was hit with a $97 million risk adjustment payment in 2015 and the expected backstop of risk corridor did not materialize, the family was forced to wind down the company and sell off the remnants. Tragically, in the midst of this debacle, Myerson took her life.

Driven by intense anger at CMS over their loss, the family reached out to attorneys in Miami to consider filing suit against CMS to get back most of the risk adjustment payment they had made—the risk corridor payments that they were legally owed would pay only 12 cents on the dollar. As part of this effort, an expert accountant was engaged and produced a very strong report that was supported by accounting rules. These attorneys approached us to see about collaborating on our respective cases (theirs was more difficult to win because it required clawing back payments already made and entailed going to a federal claims court for a decision). Seeing no downside to sharing our resources and evidence, we gave the okay for our attorneys to talk with them.

Early the following week, we had our regular weekly conference call with our CMS project officer, which provided us with a pitiful sort of comic interlude. Just recently, we had been assigned to Janice—after Thomas, and, before him, Maureen. Well-meaning, but poorly informed and completely powerless, these representatives were required to ask us the same six or seven questions every week, so the CMS higher-ups could say that they were appropriately overseeing the CO-OPs. Part of our conference call follows:

Janice: "What plans do you have if your enrollment is over your original estimate of 53,000 by the end of the year?"

Peter: "We don't need a plan; the risk adjustment debacle has scared off the brokers, causing us to lose out on new cases, so we've revised our estimated year-end enrollment to be about 45,000—if we even exist by then, thanks to risk adjustment."

J: "So, no plans for over-enrollment?"

P: "No."

J: "How do you plan to address your high risk adjustment payment?"

P: "We sued CMS."

J: "I see; what contingency plans do you have to deal with risk adjustment?"

P: "We're suing CMS."

J and Maureen: "Tell us about the lawsuit."

P: "We're suing CMS."

J: "I hear your frustration. CMS leadership shares your frustration."

P: "With all due respect, CMS leadership is responsible for the mess, could solve the problem with the stroke of a pen, and doesn't care about this problem at all."

J: "I will take this back to the leadership."

P: "That's great."

J: "Next week, I look forward to an update on the lawsuit."

On the loan front, Evergreen was still in a holding pattern regarding firming up guarantors. It had become clear to us that we needed a minimum of $8 million, which would allow us to stay above 200% risk-based capital, and thus avoid action by the Maryland Insurance Administration. A $15 million loan would be sufficient, allowing us to stay in the high 300% range of RBC, and $20 million would be ample, keeping us at our current level of 500% RBC. Having received a tentative no from the Casey Foundation, we still were waiting on the Abell Foundation, the State of Maryland's Venture Fund, the Massachusetts CO-OP, and George Soros.

Throughout the last week of June, a lot of action occurred on the legal front, as we went over the affidavits that would be filed with the request for a preliminary injunction at the end of the month. There would be at least three such documents, the most comprehensive of which would be mine. The other two were from our actuarial expert, David Axene, and our whistleblower.

Axene's first attempt at his testimony laid out a framework of how flawed the risk adjustment formula and methodology were, making the point that there were plenty of good examples of very effective risk adjustment methodologies that CMS could have drawn from, but chose not to do so. The major points in his testimony—which mirrored our claims about the fatal flaws of the CMS methodology—were helpful to our case, but they were stated in such a way that I had trouble clearly understanding them. Carolyn Brown and Phil Peisch had a similar difficulty, so we asked Axene to revise the testimony and put his comments more in layman's terms.

By the end of June, we had the first drafts of both the memorandum supporting a preliminary injunction (which made the legal case for our request for a PI) and of my affidavit. After going through a few edits, the case was looking fairly strong. However, we did suffer a setback when Phil informed us that our whistleblower had declined to sign his affidavit, which outlined what he had told us about CMS's approach to risk adjustment. Phil reassured us that, even if the affidavit from the whistleblower never made it to the judge, we had a pretty solid case without it—and there was always a risk that there was something we did not know about our informer, especially given the tight timetable, which precluded us from doing more thorough vetting.

Still, it was unfortunate that the whistleblower had bailed out, since his draft affidavit was quite strong, and came awfully close to proving that the decisions made by CMS regarding the risk adjustment methodology were indeed arbitrary.

The day before the release of the risk adjustment assessments for insurers across the country, we got an email from CMS regarding the upcoming notification, stating that they would be sending out notice of their respective risk adjustment assessments to all insurers between 4 p.m. and 5 p.m. EDT, the next afternoon, June 30.

At this juncture, we had three options for survival:

- The case for the preliminary injunction regarding our payment was solid, with an affidavit from an expert actuary, Evergreen's affidavit, congressional testimony and emails from Al Redmer, the strong legal arguments from the Florida insurer's expert actuary, and concrete evidence of CMS's admission that there were serious flaws in its methodology. We certainly had a strong response to the requirement that we would suffer irreparable damage should we be forced to make the payment. It would come down to the defense mounted by the US Department of Justice attorneys and our response to their case.
- In addition, we were about halfway to the desired $15 million in loan guarantees. So far, we tentatively had $3 million from Massachusetts's CO-OP; $2.5 million from the State of Maryland's Department of Commerce; and $1 million from the Abell Foundation. We were still waiting to hear about a possible $10 million guarantee from George Soros or a lesser amount from his foundation; and we were going back to the Maryland Department of Commerce for an additional $2.5 million. We now had until about July 15 to firm up the additional $5 million or so that would satisfy the MIA that we would have a large enough loan to cover most of our $20 million loss from risk adjustment if we didn't win the preliminary injunction.
- On the third option—finding a buyer for the CO-OP, it was obvious to Manny and me that no investor in their right mind would be interested in buying out our CMS loan and injecting additional capital to allow for growth until the risk adjustment issue had been addressed—either by a successful lawsuit or by securing an adequate loan. Thus, pursuing a buyer for Evergreen would be Part 2 of our survival plan.

The morning of June 30, we got the near-final drafts of the two affidavits (David Axene's actuarial brief and my declaration) and the entire memorandum supporting the preliminary injunction. I spent the day making changes and sending them back and forth to Phil. I was quite pleased with how the case was being presented—our attorneys did a great job in making our points, and did so in a very accessible manner, considering the complexity of the issue.

At 4:00 p.m. we started watching our email inbox for the imminent risk adjustment announcement. After staring at our inbox for about twenty minutes, Manny called his colleague at the Maine CO-OP, who told him the information would be out at 4:30. Four-thirty came and went, as did 5:00, with no email from CMS. Then, at 5:10, I started getting calls from reporters who had downloaded the link to all the risk adjustment payments that had been sent to them by CMS. I found out our payment from a reporter rather than CMS: a staggering $24.2 million, even more devastating than we had anticipated.

The total damage to the CO-OPs was stunning—the ten remaining CO-OPs owed a combined total risk adjustment payment of $143 million to competitors in their own states. After spending the next half hour looking over the report detailing the payment or receivable for every insurer in each state, a pattern became clear. With very few exceptions, the big winner in virtually every state was the local Blue Cross / Blue Shield entity. By my calculations, the Blues nationwide received a total of $1.5 billion from their competitors. Maryland paralleled that trend, with Evergreen's $24 million all going to CareFirst, and CareFirst netting an additional $26 million in total receivables from other insurers in the state. Of course, CMS tried to put a good spin on the results, but to no avail. The next morning, the first headlines from industry and political publications blasted CMS. This from *Modern Healthcare* was typical: "BREAKING: ACA's risk adjustment hammers small plans again."

As I looked through the entire CMS report on the winners and losers of the risk adjustment assessments, it struck me that we should ask the judge to perform an "outrageousness test." Putting aside the legal arguments on our side, he could just ask himself if the results pass the smell test. It reminded me of former Supreme Court Associate Justice Potter Stewart's opinion on the definition of pornography: "I know it when I see it." Of course it was a pipe dream, but I wanted the judge in our case to come to the same conclusion about the outrageousness of the risk adjustment process. That outrageousness should lead to a finding that CMS's risk adjustment methodology was indeed arbitrary and capricious, and therefore unlawful.

Over the next several days, headline after headline made our case that the new small entrants were severely disadvantaged by risk adjustment. A couple of examples: "ObamaCare Just Killed Its Lowest-Cost Insurers; Premiums to Rise Further," by Jed Graham, *Investor's Business Daily*; and "Is a co-op collapse coming?," by Dan Diamond, *Politico Pulse*.

By July 5, the first casualties of the recently released risk adjustment assessments occurred. First, Illinois's CO-OP, Land of Lincoln, was effectively shut down, followed by Connecticut's. The latter case was particularly troubling. Its CEO, Ken Lalime, was, along with me and two others, one of the only remaining original CO-OP CEOs. He was a genuinely good guy—with a very solid staff. In addition, their risk adjustment payment was only $13.3 million, with an enrollment similar to ours. Granted, they were not yet profitable, as we were, but their insurance commissioner took them into receivership for being in a financial state that might actually have been better than ours.

In a conversation after his Connecticut CO-OP had been shuttered, Lalime lamented what could have been had CMS been a better partner to the CO-OPs —in terms of providing capital and promulgating fairer policies. Ken thought that the CO-OPs, as originally conceived, would have been the saving grace for the ACA—"if there were fifty strong home-grown, patient-centered, high quality 'better mousetraps' built in each state, after four to six years the feds could take them over, per statute, and would have been handed fifty individualized public option nonprofits." He felt strongly that the CO-OPs only needed one more year of capital to keep them viable until the risk adjustment process settled out. "But," he told me, "we didn't have the capital that the big guys had to survive the initial tumult . . . and the risk stability programs killed us—risk adjustment charges cut off one leg, and the lack of risk corridor receivables was the knife in the back."

The Connecticut insurance commissioner, Katharine Wade, in her public comments also criticized CMS/HHS directly for refusing to change: "Commissioner Wade and her staff have expressed their concerns to federal authorities over the risk adjustment formula and its potentially damaging effects on the market, particularly its impact on small insurers like HealthyCT. Together with her fellow regulators, Commissioner Wade has personally met with HHS Secretary Burwell to seek a more workable market stabilization mechanism. Unfortunately, the federal Center for Medicare and Medicaid Services ('CMS') has declined to modify its approach for the 2017 plan year."

As these were only the first two states taking quick action after the risk adjustment assessments came out, one might have hoped that such criticisms would get CMS to amend the process to prevent further elimination of competitors in additional markets. But that would be giving CMS credit for some degree of flexibility.

I heard from a source that our commissioner was getting antsy about our situation and was spooked by the actions of his colleagues in Illinois and Connecticut, so I called Commissioner Redmer to update him on our actions. First, I tried to confirm that if we won the preliminary injunction, we would be in the clear. He thought so, but still wasn't positive that we could take the liability off our books, resulting in too little in reserves. However, he seemed willing to be flexible about that, especially if we won a PI against both the payment and the assessment (if it couldn't be assessed, then we wouldn't have to book it).

More concerning was his contention that we had to have the loans completed by August 15. We were still stuck at about $6.5 million in guarantees for a secured loan; however, we also were now actively in pursuit of an unsecured loan. Several investors who were interested in a buyout of Evergreen from CMS seemed willing to help, if they got the first right of refusal on the main deal.

We thought that, going forward, these points would help to reassure the MIA, but shortly after I discussed them with Redmer, we received an ominous email from one of his deputies stating that the loan(s) would have to be finalized by August 1, so that the lenders and terms of the loan could be vetted by August 15 (which was looking more like D-Day), and that we had to submit financial documents demonstrating that our solvency level was adequate. Time was running out.

At the end of the day I called our lead attorney, Caroline Brown, to inform her of recent developments and to see if it was possible to ask for an expedited hearing on our preliminary injunction. It seemed to me that it would be better to have the hearing in July, as I wasn't sure that we'd still be in business in early August, when the case would otherwise be heard. She asked for the recent email from the MIA and more information on Connecticut's actions, as these would be used to make the case for expedited review to prevent imminent irreparable harm.

At the end of the first week of July, we had a meeting with the board of the PCOs, to go over contingency planning should Evergreen CO-OP go under.

Since the CO-OP supplied 90% of the patients to the PCOs, the ramifications of a CO-OP failure were potentially catastrophic for the PCOs. Liz Burger, the new executive director of the PCOs, did a great job of putting together the options for the board.

What could have been a melancholy meeting turned out to be a very productive discussion. One of the options for Evergreen CO-OP's survival was to sell itself to an investor to get out from the CMS loan, and to pay off the risk adjustment debt. Very possibly the investor would be interested in rolling the PCOs into the deal as well. This seemed like a great outcome, with the PCOs' $6 million line of credit being paid off and the potential of permanently linking the two entities in one corporate structure. If the CO-OP went completely out of business, the PCOs could be sold to a healthcare system or hospital. However, the geographic spread of the PCOs made it unlikely that a single system would take all four, and the patient panel of each center—currently about 2,000, so we could provide great care—was less than the number of patients seen by a single physician in the typical primary care setting. We considered several other options, and the meeting closed with a request to Liz Burger and me to make a list of actions that would need to be taken as soon as the CO-OP's fate was known in early August.

Chapter Eight

Evergreen Health Cooperative v. United States of America

July 2016

With the release of the risk adjustment payment likely to result in our imminent demise, we asked Judge George Russell for the option of expediting the hearing on our motion for a preliminary injunction, so that a decision on that motion would be made before August 1. Our case for the expedited PI was made much stronger by the inclusion of numerous articles about small new entrants all over the country being hammered by the large payables assessed by CMS the previous week. These articles also noted that, within a week of the announcement, several small and rapidly growing carriers, due to the faulty risk adjustment methodology, were being shut down and put under control of state insurance departments as the first step to being completely closed by the end of the year.

Shortly thereafter, I got a call from Chris Lynch, Senator Ben Cardin's chief of staff, who informed me that he was sending me a copy of a note that HHS Secretary Sylvia Burwell had sent to the senator, responding to his concerns about risk adjustment and Evergreen. In essence, Burwell was under the impression that the states now had legal authority to ease the transition to the new health insurance markets of the Affordable Care Act. She also noted that

CMS encouraged states to look at any local approaches that might be necessary.

Well—where to start? As Al Redmer had told me several times, CMS was completely unyielding in its refusal to approve any option proposed by the Maryland Insurance Administration. As far as we knew, not a single option proposed by any state to remediate outrageous risk adjustment payments had been approved by CMS. Secretary Burwell's understanding of the situation thus was incorrect.

Midday, our attorneys at Covington and Burling filed our request for an expedited hearing on our PI. Shortly thereafter, I called Al Redmer to let him know of this development. I took the opportunity to make a new ask: since we now knew that we were owed $18.345 million from the 2015 *risk corridor program* (plus an additional $2 million for 2014), could we offset that $20-plus million against our $24-plus million risk adjustment payment on our books, knowing that the risk corridor money was very unlikely to be released due to congressional action? "Not without us putting you under supervision," Redmer replied.

Meanwhile, Phil Peisch had talked to the Department of Justice litigator, Matthew Lawrence, regarding the timing of the hearing. Both parties now agreed that an expedited hearing on the PI made sense, and we presented this to Judge George Russell, who had been assigned our case.

As another CO-OP (this time from Oregon, leaving only seven survivors) was being shut down immediately, there continued to be a lot of articles on the negative impact of risk adjustment on the CO-OPs' fates. Several of them had good analyses of the issue, and we sent them directly to Peisch and Caroline Brown for potential use in our arguments against the government. I even copied comments President Obama had made in his article on the ACA's impact in *JAMA* to make one of our points: that one of the major goals of the ACA was to foster new competition.

Peisch notified us that the hearing on our motion for a preliminary injunction had been scheduled for the next Tuesday, July 19, only six days hence. It seemed that Judge Russell was scheduled to go on vacation for the last week of July and the first week of August. He clearly recognized the time-sensitive nature of our complaint—a good sign—and gave us the first date possible. Interestingly, the lead DOJ attorney acquiesced to the government filing their brief in two days, leaving us the upcoming weekend to develop our responses to their arguments. Our rebuttal was due on Monday, the day before the hearing. Simply getting a hearing was also a positive sign—had the case been a slam dunk for the government, the judge would likely have simply read the briefs and published his decision.

Finally, it seemed that CMS's dismissive behavior regarding the CO-OPs was starting to come back to haunt them. First, the domino-like failures of the remaining CO-OPs had become a constant drumbeat in the media, even making the CNN "news ticker" one evening. This coverage led to a new avenue for an indictment of the ACA, generating renewed congressional interest in the CO-OP issue. Smelling blood (and media coverage), three committees had reopened investigations into the failed CO-OPs. A hearing of a subcommittee of the House Oversight and Government Reform Committee came first. For over an hour, the number two official of CMS, Kevin Counihan, was verbally pounded by the subcommittee members for CMS's unresponsiveness to congressional requests for information, for their lack of oversight of the CO-OPs, and for their attitude.

Meanwhile, Peisch informed us that Judge Russell had all but telegraphed his opinion on one aspect of our case—that there were grounds for a PI based on the likelihood of irreparable damage. Russell had gone so far as to tell the DOJ attorney that he couldn't imagine why they wouldn't simply concede that point at the outset. The US attorney didn't acquiesce on that point, but did agree not to ask for an extension, and he would allow our actuarial expert and me to testify at the hearing, along with oral arguments presented by the two sets of lawyers.

The only bad news was that George Soros had declined our request for a $10 million loan guarantee. That basically ruled out a fully guaranteed loan to get us over the risk adjustment payment if we had to pony up. On the other hand, it was looking more and more as if this bridge loan would be part of a bigger deal with an investor group, and the lack of a guaranteed loan made our case for irreparable damage even stronger.

At the end of the day, I updated Al Redmer on all our efforts and where we stood. Pleased to be kept in the loop, he wished us luck in nailing down a solution.

CMS/HHS's Department of Justice attorney called our lawyers midday on July 15 to tell them to "hold the presses." CMS was proposing a new policy that they thought would eliminate the need for Tuesday's hearing. Apparently, they had already proposed it to the MIA. I immediately called Al Redmer to see what weighty proposal had been made. He replied that the assessment would continue, but CMS would allow Evergreen to pay the $24 million back over a few months. This was nothing new, and he couldn't believe the government would think that it would be even remotely acceptable to us—because, as the feds knew full well, if we had to book the assessment, our solvency level would become legally insufficient and we would be put into receivership on August 15, period.

Clearly, with this gambit CMS was trying to avert the hearing on Tuesday. One could only assume they were worried about the ramifications, both in Maryland and nationally, if we won an injunction. It would throw the risk adjustment payment transfer out of balance in Maryland and set a precedent that might induce other insurers negatively affected by risk adjustment to take similar legal action in their respective federal courts. The whole risk adjustment system could be thrown into chaos.

In a small-world situation, Nancy-Ann DeParle (formerly of the White House) was now a partner in the private equity firm we were pitching the following Monday about purchasing Evergreen, and she gave me a call. After some introductory talk about our backgrounds and an interesting tidbit from her about my earlier email passed to her by Jim Messina (she had indeed taken our issue to the White House—though not to the president—and she was told in no uncertain terms that the White House was ceding any decisions about the risk adjustment issue to HHS and CMS), she told me of her recent discussions with CMS about the possibility of a CO-OP being converted to a for-profit by investors. CMS had told her they would only allow this if the CO-OP was in the process of being wound down (that is, in receivership to be liquidated). However, this approach would effectively allow for a private equity firm to get the assets of a failed CO-OP at fire-sale prices. Then the firm could take off with the remains to turn them into a profit-generating entity with the taxpayers likely getting nothing in return. Wouldn't it make far more sense for CMS to allow an existing, potentially viable CO-OP to be sold to investors who would at least pay off the CMS loan at some cents on the dollar, thereby generating some payback for the taxpayers who had footed the original loan? This intriguing idea loomed as a possibility for us.

Just before midnight on Friday, the government attorneys filed their brief countering our motion for a preliminary injunction. I read it cursorily before going to bed—planning to get up early Saturday to delve into their arguments in detail. But before I got off the computer, I saw an email from Caroline Brown. The DOJ lawyer had notified her that CMS had just posted a new policy that might eliminate the need for Tuesday's hearing. It was apparently a later version of the new policy we had looked into earlier in the day. It basically laid out the circumstances in which a company could net or offset certain monies owed to it against the risk adjustment payments they would have to make. In the list of charges that could be netted were risk adjustment and risk corridor. If that was truly the case, we would be in great shape, but I didn't trust CMS for one minute. Or, could this be the agency caving due to pressure from our lawsuit?

The description of the new policy—less than a page in length—was so opaque that even our extremely talented lawyers couldn't understand it. So, while waiting for a response from DOJ on exactly what the new CMS policy said, the Covington team and Mary, Manny, and I spent Saturday morning on a conference call going over the government's arguments.

The vast majority of the government's fifty-page brief was spent contending that we did not actually face imminent irreparable harm. They tried to support this claim by (a) using newspaper quotes against us, in which I had said we were hopeful of getting financing in time to avert receivership; (b) claiming that Al Redmer wasn't really going to place us into receivership on August 15; (c) arguing that if we were really in such dire straits, why hadn't we sued earlier; and (d) declaring that we were late to the game because we hadn't known how bad our charge would be.

We had always felt that showing imminent irreparable harm was the easiest hurdle to get over, so we were pleased that the government's case focused primarily on that issue. The answers to the government's case against imminent irreparable harm were: (a) financing wouldn't be obtained in time; (b) Al Redmer was definitely going to put us into receivership on August 15, absent an injunction or miraculous financing; (c) we had only pursued litigation against the federal government as a last resort, after expending immense effort to get the faulty methodology changed; and (d) we had been working for close to a year with CMS/HHS, Congress, the White House, and the MIA to amend the risk adjustment process, when we expected our charge to be only a few million dollars.

DOJ's brief spent little time defending against our claim that the methodology was arbitrary—they claimed that it was a reasonable attempt to determine the health or sickness of a carrier's population. Unlike our brief, which included an affidavit from expert actuaries, DOJ did not make much of a case on the appropriateness of the formula and process. However, by law, the burden of proof on this claim was squarely on our shoulders, because the federal Administrative Procedure Act clearly gave wide latitude to federal agencies in promulgating rules. In other words, being stupid or incompetent didn't make a rule arbitrary and capricious. The agency had to have known that there was a good chance the process wasn't going to accomplish what it was intended to. To prove the latter point, we were relying on our actuarial expert.

The government's case barely addressed our second claim—that risk corridors and risk adjustment were part and parcel of the same formula. Nor did it say anything much about our third claim—that the federal government had overreached by running risk adjustment rather than letting the states do it—saying simply that since Maryland hadn't chosen to run risk adjustment in state, the feds therefore had the right to do so.

Friday morning, I headed to Washington for a prep session with Peisch and Brown. In their beautiful high-windowed offices, Phil took me through all the questions he was going to ask during my testimony on Tuesday. In addition to questions about my educational and professional background, he asked when we had become aware of the threat of risk adjustment; what efforts we had taken to change the process; and finally, what threats were imminent if we didn't get an injunction.

Figuring out exactly how to answer the questions posed was an interesting process. For example, in response to Phil's question about what efforts I had made to get the risk adjustment process changed, I initially told him everything I had done: meeting with Andy Slavitt and HHS; letters and phone calls to CMS; enlisting our entire congressional delegation, especially Senator Cardin and Congressman Elijah Cummings to get to the secretary of HHS; getting former high-ranking Obama officials to approach the White House; and talking to other congressional staff from other states. However, Caroline noted that if I answered that way, the judge might conclude that we didn't have a very good argument, if all those high-powered officials we had enlisted to help us couldn't persuade little old CMS. Her suggestion was to focus on our many efforts with CMS, and Al Redmer's multiple approaches to CMS, and to highlight CMS's intransigence and unreasonableness.

After three hours of preparing I felt decently confident that I could pull off a serviceable performance on the witness stand.

Brown and Peisch came up to Baltimore on Tuesday morning, July 19, to do some last-minute prepping on my testimony, our actuary's testimony, and Caroline's oral arguments. At 12:30, we left Evergreen for the federal courthouse in downtown Baltimore—a 1970s-style concrete eyesore. After taking the elevator to the seventh floor, we got a great panoramic view of Baltimore through the large windows while walking to courtroom 7A.

Caroline Brown, Phil Peisch, Mary Porter, and I took our seats at the plaintiff's table, a little before two, and in a short while the judge entered the courtroom. Judge George Levi Russell III was the son of a well-known, groundbreaking African American attorney in Baltimore. Judge Russell had served as a Baltimore City Circuit Court judge, and for the last four years had served as a Federal District Court judge in the District of Maryland. Our attorneys didn't know much about him in advance, although his relatively recent ascent to the federal bench gave them some pause about his willingness to rule against the federal government, as opposed to longer-serving jurists, who might not show as much deference to the government.

The judge seemed to be a pleasant fellow, gave introductory remarks, and then directed Peisch to call his first witness: me.

My testimony was relatively uneventful. The two prep sessions definitely helped to reduce my nervousness on the stand. The questions from Peisch proceeded as we had practiced—my background; Evergreen's history, philosophy, and model of care; followed by the harm that would result if Evergreen were to be shuttered due to risk adjustment. Here, I think we made a very strong case. I first countered the government's contention that an injunction would destabilize the Maryland marketplace because CareFirst wouldn't get their payment, by pointing out that our payment to CareFirst amounted to a rounding error for the gigantic insurer, and, if we were closed, CareFirst would not get paid the $24 million anyway. I then talked about the disruption to our almost 40,000 members, who would have to find new insurance at the end of the year (in the best-case scenario of a wind-down) or lose their insurance immediately, potentially threatening their health (in the worst-case scenario of an immediate liquidation).

Additionally, the 7,000-plus Evergreen members using our PCOs as their primary care provider would lose their source of excellent care, and as Maryland has a dearth of primary care physicians, would likely have a hard time being seen or even finding a new primary care provider. Of course, I pointed out the harm to our dedicated staff (many of whom were in the courtroom)—all 105 CO-OP and PCO employees would lose their jobs.

Judge Russell did ask me directly why we hadn't considered the possibility of a big risk adjustment payment, and if there wasn't a risk inherent in simply being a startup. I was able to defuse the first comment to some extent by pointing out that the best actuaries in the country had been unable to predict risk adjustment payments with any accuracy. On the second, I think I impressed him when I informed him that in only our third year of existence, we were actually profitable without the unmerited risk adjustment payment. My testimony concluded with the point that our demise would also result in harm to the entire Maryland health insurance market—loss of competition, less consumer choice, and less innovation—all of which were completely antithetical to the major goals of the ACA.

On cross-examination, DOJ's lead attorney prodded me a bit about when we first became aware of the threat of risk adjustment, and what we had done about it, but the questions were innocuous and didn't seem damaging in the least, and so I was excused.

At this point it seemed very likely that we had passed the first test necessary to get a preliminary injunction—demonstrating imminent irreparable damage. Now, to pass the second test and buy us additional time to make a comprehensive deal, we had to persuade Judge Russell that we were likely to succeed in a full trial on the merits of at least one of our substantive claims.

Next up was our actuary, who had flown east from Southern California to testify. However, after he had been sworn in and asked a few questions about his background, the judge halted the proceedings and called all the attorneys up to the bench. Since I was at the plaintiff's table, I could use the headphones provided, allowing me to listen in to the discussion. What transpired caused me a great deal of concern. The judge informed our lawyers that he was not going to allow the upcoming testimony because he felt that the actuary would be testifying on his opinion only on the *legitimacy* of the risk adjustment methodology, not on the *process* by which it was developed. It was clear from his comments, that Judge Russell had a very strict reading of the Administrative Procedure Act—the 1946 federal law that gave enormous latitude to federal agencies in developing the rules and regulations necessary to meet the requirements of legislation.

This leeway allowed for poorly constructed rules—even those demonstrably destructive or stupid—as long as the process of rule-making took into account important issues. This requirement had been imposed to prevent an unending steam of potentially frivolous lawsuits against federal agencies every time a rule was released with which an affected entity disagreed. Thus, Judge Russell's decision to not allow Axene's testimony made it clear to us that the first claim in our lawsuit against the federal government—that the risk adjustment methodology was arbitrary and capricious—did not hold much water for him. That left us with our risk adjustment / risk corridor offset argument to convince Judge Russell that we had a likelihood of winning the eventual case on the merits of at least one claim.

Caroline Brown did a masterful job in her oral argument, making our case that the risk adjustment and risk corridors went hand in hand by statute. If you owed one and the government owed you on the other, the payments should be netted. In other words, you should not be on the hook to the government if they weren't going to offset what they owed you.

The judge even used Brown's points to challenge the DOJ attorney to respond to our claim. First, DOJ tried to argue that this was a request for federal funds, which would require that we file the case in the US Court of Federal Claims, but the judge didn't buy that since all we were asking for was a netting of funds, not new funds. Then DOJ argued, with convoluted logic and no real evidence, that the government had three years before they had to make risk corridor payments. Challenged again by Judge Russell as to the veracity of that point, the DOJ attorney became even more flustered and quickly finished his comments, without offering a logical rationale for this contention. Judge Russell did not seem to be impressed with DOJ's arguments on this aspect of the case, which gave us some hope he might find that we had a likelihood of prevailing on the merits of the risk adjustment / risk corridor claim.

By 4:30 p.m., arguments were complete, and we all listened with bated breath as Judge Russell prepared to speak. Quietly, he informed the room that he was taking the case under advisement and he would give his decision in person Thursday at 11:30 a.m. With that, the hearing was adjourned. According to Brown and Peisch, this was an unusual development because generally judges released their decisions electronically. What this meant was anyone's guess, so we had to wait about forty-eight hours to learn our fate.

Early Wednesday morning, the Evergreen team got on a conference call with the Covington team to go over contingency plans. We all agreed that, although we clearly seemed to have overcome the initial hurdle of proving imminent irreparable harm, it was very unlikely that we had convinced the judge that we could win the claim about the risk adjustment methodology being arbitrary and capricious. On the other hand, we were cautiously optimistic that we might prevail on the risk adjustment / risk corridor offset issue. To that end, Brown and Peisch had found strong evidence in favor of our argument that risk corridor payments were due before three years had passed, and more importantly, as we pointed out later in a letter to Judge Russell, CMS's actual policy of making prompt payment of risk corridor was clearly stated in two regulatory documents.

Thinking that the DOJ lawyers were concerned that we might prevail, we decided on a settlement offer that Brown would make to CMS/DOJ. We would ask for a ninety-day abatement of the risk adjustment payment and assessment and for a good faith effort from CMS to approve a private equity deal (with an entity that would agree to buy Evergreen and pay off the risk adjustment assessment as part of the deal), which we would bring to them within those ninety days, after which the payment would be due.

Brown took our proposal to DOJ that morning, and their response was a curt one-sentence email from the lead DOJ attorney informing us that CMS would not agree to it. Phil Peisch notified us of CMS's decision and added the following note:

> CMS has rejected our suggestion that we come to an agreement to delay everything until October 30. Caroline and I had a quick call with the DOJ lawyers, in which Caroline forcefully made the case that even a judgment in CMS's favor tomorrow would give the agency a "black eye"—CMS would not get its risk adjustment payment, another co-op in receivership, decrease market competition in Maryland, etc. She explained that this is the stage in litigation when DOJ, as CMS's lawyers, really needs to "bang heads" to make something work and explain to CMS that it makes no sense to not agree to a modest delay. DOJ lawyers said they would go back to CMS again to see if something could be worked out, but given their tone I do not think we'll hear anything positive back from them.

Now that we knew there would be no settlement, we considered our other options, should we not get an injunction. We quickly decided that we would appeal a negative decision to the US Court of Appeals for the Fourth Circuit —after all, there was nothing to lose—especially because recent case law favored a broader read of the Administrative Procedure Act than Judge Russell apparently had.

On Thursday, July 21, seated at the plaintiff's table again, I closed my eyes as we awaited the judge's appearance at 11:30 a.m. With Caroline Brown, Phil Peisch, and Mary Porter seated next to me, I went through the case, to see if there was anything we could have done better—but nothing came to mind. My solitude was abruptly interrupted by the clerk's pronouncement: "All rise."

The judge launched into a recitation of his decision—one that would take a full forty minutes to deliver. Starting with the facts of the case, he covered the passage of the ACA and the history of Evergreen, before turning to the question of irreparable harm. As we had hoped, he quickly proclaimed that we had passed that hurdle. However, in order to be granted a preliminary injunction, we also had to prove that we had a reasonable likelihood to prevail on at least one of our claims. Before such a ruling, Judge Russell briefly laid out the rationale for the development of the three Rs of the ACA (risk adjustment, risk corridor, and reinsurance) as a mechanism to stabilize the marketplaces with the introduction of a new system of coverage.

He then turned to claim #1—that the risk adjustment methodology was arbitrary and capricious. Although he acknowledged that CMS's development of the formula was obviously flawed, and the results of the risk adjustment process were grossly unfair, the facts of the case made it very difficult to overcome the tremendous deference granted to the government by the Administrative Procedure Act. As he had telegraphed during the hearing (when he hadn't allowed our expert actuarial witness to testify), Judge Russell ruled that because CMS had at least considered certain critical components for the formula—for example, pharmacy claims, though they weren't ultimately used—their actions were faulty, but not arbitrary or capricious.

Skipping over claim #2, he then turned to claim #3 of our case—that CMS had usurped the state's role as the entity charged with administering the risk adjustment process. I had always felt that this was our weakest claim. The judge came to the same conclusion, pointing out that the state had had an opportunity to run risk adjustment in Maryland but had chosen not to, and therefore the federal government had a right to do so. Again, we weren't surprised.

Our staff and our attorneys at the table displayed looks of cautious optimism, as the judge had left our best claim for last, and appeared to be leading up to a theatrical conclusion. Our confidence rose as he gave a supportive summation of our arguments on claim #2—that we should be able to offset our risk adjustment payment with risk corridor receivables. He stated that the intent of Congress was clearly to have risk adjustment and risk corridor go hand in hand, and that the magnitude of one affected the calculation of the other, just as we had asserted. Victory at hand! But just before it seemed as though he was leading up to granting us the preliminary injunction, he veered off track. Using logic that I didn't follow, he argued that even though the intent of Congress was for the programs to be intertwined, CMS nonetheless was tasked with administration of the risk corridor program and could do so as it saw fit. If they didn't have enough funds to pay risk corridor right now, CMS either could delay it or not pay it entirely. "Therefore," the judge concluded, "the emergency preliminary injunctive relief requested will be denied as to this claim."

After acknowledging that the issues ruled on were important enough to be reviewed, he gave his approval to immediately appeal the case to the Fourth Circuit. He then closed the case by commenting, "I'm going to say this was a very difficult case for the court to end up having to decide. It was extraordinarily well-presented, and I want to thank both counsels for that. Thank you."

"All rise," the clerk intoned, as Judge Russell stepped down from the bench, and, just like that, it was over.

Stunned, the Covington folks and our team adjourned to the hallway. First, Brown sought out the DOJ attorneys and Van Dorsey, the MIA counsel, to see if any delay of the assessment could be worked out to the satisfaction of the MIA. Dorsey said he couldn't make that call.

In fact, the entire staff of the MIA, except Al Redmer, had seemingly soured on us. While on site at Evergreen, auditing us earlier in the week, several members had made comments about how they were just about ready to come in and put us into receivership. With administrative options closing rapidly, we now had only two avenues left to pursue to keep us alive: an appeal of today's decision, and obtaining a loan—quickly.

As we had already decided that we would appeal a negative decision, Peisch and Brown headed back to DC to work on the brief for the appeal, with plans to call us about the emphasis of the case later that afternoon. In that call, we decided we would focus our appeal solely on the risk adjustment / risk corridor offset issue, because there was a much lower burden of proof on this claim compared to the "arbitrary and capricious" claim about risk adjustment methodology, and because Judge Russell had walked right up to the line on granting a PI on this aspect of our case. He'd left us a hook on which to hang our argument: his apparently contradictory logic that the intent of Congress was clearly to have risk adjustment and risk corridors go hand in hand, including the calculation of payment, and yet CMS could do what they wished with risk corridors. That didn't make sense to us—if Congress's will was thwarted by the agency tasked with implementing it, then CMS was in the wrong and should be required to offset the risk adjustment payable and risk corridor receivable.

We planned to file the appeal Saturday, July 23, which would allow the Fourth Circuit to decide on the PI by the end of the week. It was a long shot, but there was nothing to lose by doing so.

The day after the ruling in district court, our attorneys sent us the draft of the brief for the appellate court. It was focused almost exclusively on claim #2, was extremely well-written, and was even more compelling than the original complaint, in part, because Brown and Peisch had heard both CMS's arguments at the hearing and the judge's comments.

The brief was very persuasive, boiling down what could have been a very arcane dispute to the crux of the matter, as stated in the preamble of the brief:

> The Government argues that Evergreen Health must annually make full risk adjustment payments to the Centers for Medicare & Medicaid Services ("CMS"), but that CMS need not annually comply with its intertwined statutory risk corridors obligations to Evergreen Health. The Government does not dispute that it has failed to make full 2014 risk corridors payments to Evergreen Health; it does not dispute that it will not make any 2015 risk corridors payments to Evergreen Health this year; it does not dispute that it requires Evergreen Health to annually make its full risk adjustment payments to CMS; and it does not dispute that CMS's offset practices treat risk corridors payments entirely differently than all other ACA payments made between the Government and health insurance issu-

ers. Rather, the Government argues that its own financial considerations justify a delay in honoring its risk corridors obligations to Evergreen Health, without any corresponding delay for the company's risk adjustment liability to CMS—not even a temporary delay that would permit Evergreen Health to secure additional financing so that it can avoid receivership and remain in business. This position is entirely inconsistent with the ACA's purpose, intent and design.

Since the government had already filed its response to our appeal, the case could be decided at any time.

Thus, for the next few days, at least every half hour or so between routine calls, I would go onto the website of the Fourth Circuit Court of Appeals, click on "daily opinions," and scan the underlying decisions that had been announced. Not seeing Evergreen v. US Department of Health and Human Services on the list by Friday, I called Caroline Brown to see what was up. She had just called the clerk of the court, who had informed her that they knew the case had to be decided by Monday, August 1, but the decision had not yet been reached. Just before six, I got an email from Phil Peisch that the decision would not come today. He reassured us that no news was not necessarily bad news. In fact, if the appellate court was going to rule against us and affirm the decision of the district court, it would likely be conveyed quickly and without much if any written opinion. On the other hand, if they were to rule for us and reverse Judge Russell's decision, they would certainly do so with a written opinion that fully laid out their reasoning. But, as we had learned, there was no predicting any of this, so we waited to hear sometime over the weekend.

By Monday morning, there was still no news from the court of appeals. Our attorneys called the clerk, who assured her that a decision would be forthcoming. Peisch and Brown called me a couple of hours later. In a somber voice, Caroline informed me that our appeal had been denied. The three-judge panel gave absolutely no rationale for the decision of the court—the order read as follows: "Upon consideration of submissions relative to the emergency motion for an injunction pending appeal or, in the alternative, for a temporary injunction until October 31, 2016, the court denies the motion."

Just like that, our legal options were gone. We were now down to one final lifeline—obtaining a loan to cover the risk adjustment until a deal could be reached with an investor to buy us and convert us to a for-profit, out from under the suffocating control of CMS.

Chapter Nine

The Pursuit of Investors Begins

July to October 2016

The afternoon of July 1, 2016, before the impending court hearing, Manny Sheldon and I spent a good deal of time with an investment banker, Jonathan Burklund, and his partner, Roberta Hurst, whom we had chosen to pursue a potential deal to buy out our loan from CMS. Burklund was bullish that he could attract a group of investors who would pay upward of $50 million for Evergreen. What this meant for Evergreen's future was clear. To get investors, we would have to become a for-profit enterprise.

This wasn't necessarily bad, as it would make it much easier to obtain additional capital. However, assuming we had a choice, exactly who invested in us would be crucial, to preserve our model of insurance aligned with primary care, which so many seemed to find intriguing and cutting edge. Burklund assured us that he and many of his potential investors were very knowledgeable about the healthcare field, and he bought into our model completely and understood my concerns. I reserved my right to be a bit skeptical.

For the next three months, Burklund, Hurst, Sheldon, and I reached out to more than fifty potential investors. There were several concerns for most of them: our troubled financial situation and whether it could be fixed; the tight timeline (at this point, it looked as if August 15 was Al Redmer's final deadline for obtaining additional financing), and caution about how CareFirst's political power might affect approval of a deal.

However, there was one big question that everyone had for us: If the deal gets you through the 2016 risk adjustment payment, what is to prevent a similar huge assessment next year? I wrote up a piece for our potential investors, to address those concerns.

In brief, I noted that: (a) we would have a far greater cohort of long-term members, allowing us to do a much better job of targeting high-risk patients for outreach efforts to get them to a physician to code their conditions than in previous years; (b) we would have a much smaller percentage of new members enrolling late in the year, thus giving us more time to get them to a doctor to chase their codes; and (c) we were working with a risk score optimization consultant with a proven record of targeting and identifying high-risk patients and getting them to a physician for coding.

Burklund quickly came up with a few investors who had expressed considerable interest in our deal. His top pick was Consonance Capital—a highly regarded New York–based fund, started by a physician who specialized in healthcare deals. One of the four partners was Nancy-Ann DeParle. When Consonance was contacted by Burklund, she remembered our recent email exchange regarding risk adjustment, considered us further, and—voilà—her group was interested in meeting with us.

Over the next couple of months, Burklund continued to produce prospective investors for us to pitch—but the combination of a short timeline and the uncertainty surrounding risk adjustment (both this year and in the future) continued to lead to a parade of polite declinations. With several of the prospects, we also had to overcome negative feelings about CMS—based on dealings they had had with them in the past. One of the private equity firms that turned us down did at least provide a good quote: "CMS loves to invite you to the game, but they won't ever tell you the rules."

By mid-July we were ready to make our pitch to Consonance, the private equity firm with whom we were most interested in partnering. We started with our pitch deck, but were stopped short by Ben Edmands, one of the partners. He and his colleagues, including DeParle, clearly understood the CO-OP program and had done a lot of investigating of our model and financial viability. They were fine with those aspects but wanted to discuss how we would deal with risk adjustment—both in the immediate future (they knew of the lawsuit, but wanted details) and, more importantly, in the long run. We gave them our risk adjustment remediation plan, highlighting the change in the landscape combined with better code-chasing capabilities. Another question they had was easily answered in the positive: Would our insurance commissioner oppose or put up obstacles to a deal that would convert Evergreen to a for-profit entity? (I had already talked to Redmer, and he was extremely supportive.) Seemingly satisfied, they let Burklund know that they were interested enough to plan a visit to Evergreen in Baltimore the following week.

Knowing that they would want to talk with our insurance commissioner, I called Al Redmer and asked him if he would be willing to meet with the Consonance partners. Not only was he willing, he would delay leaving for a beach vacation and even come to our headquarters for the meeting. We could not have asked for a more substantial show of support.

Consistent with the roller-coaster ride that seemed to represent the life of Evergreen, the meeting with Consonance took place the day after we had been denied the preliminary injunction in court, a huge legal setback, yet an air of (very) cautious optimism arose in the Evergreen executive suite.

Consonance spent almost five hours on site with us. The two partners who came to Evergreen were Nancy-Ann DeParle and Ben Edmands, a very pleasant, experienced private equity professional who clearly knew a lot about health insurance and healthcare in general.

First was the meeting at Evergreen with Al Redmer. The commissioner was very supportive, extolling our value to the market, strongly endorsing the plan to go for-profit and reassuring the Consonance principals about the widespread political support Evergreen enjoyed in Maryland and on Capitol Hill. By the time he left, any doubts Consonance might have had about our support from the Maryland Insurance Administration had completely evaporated. We also showed the Consonance folks one of our primary care offices, where they were able to witness firsthand the personalized, comprehensive approach to our patients at the centers.

The visit ended on a positive note—the Consonance partners expressed their appreciation for our model of care and innovative approach to the intersection of an insurance company and a system of primary/preventive care centers. They promised to complete their due diligence process as rapidly as possible—particularly regarding the potential of lower risk adjustment payments going forward—as they understood the August 15 deadline we were up against to avoid being put into receivership.

To prepare for converting to a for-profit insurance carrier, we met with Ren Tundermann, our outside regulatory counsel, to discuss how to get MIA approval for this action, which turned out to be a formidable task. Ironically, we faced this burden because of long-ago maneuvers by our biggest competitor. CareFirst had tried to convert from a not-for-profit insurer to a for-profit entity in 2003. However, they ran into opposition for many reasons, most importantly the greediness of their executive team—eight of whom stood to make over $140 million in the deal. This created a hue and cry against the transaction, and an offended state legislature passed strict restrictions on such a deal in the middle of the negotiations between CareFirst and their suitor, WellPoint.

Thus, any such deal, then and in the future, had to adhere to the following process: file an application with the Maryland insurance commissioner, which included (a) a detailed financial report on the company and officers buying the nonprofit; (b) an independent valuation of the nonprofit, with any assets required to be donated to a charitable organization providing health services; (c) a public interest study, conducted by an independent entity and showing that the conversion was in the interest of the general public; (d) proof that such a deal wouldn't create an antitrust situation; and (e) a detailed plan of how executive compensation would be handled once conversion had occurred (included in this section of the law was an outright prohibition on existing executives obtaining shares of the business—an obvious reference to the CareFirst executives' overreach).

After the application was filed, the insurance commissioner was then to hold a public hearing on the conversion, with testimony allowed from the general public. Following this quasi-legislative hearing, the commissioner was to make his decision within sixty days. Then the transaction couldn't close for ninety days, unless the legislature was in session—in which case the General Assembly had to vote its approval or disapproval of the deal.

We were fairly confident that we would not have much opposition in the hearing—certainly not anywhere near the level of antipathy that CareFirst received (a hearing in which, ironically, I testified against CareFirst as the Baltimore City Health Commissioner). We realized that we could appropriately answer the various questions asked as part of the process (that is, we could show that conversion was in the public interest as being the only viable way for Evergreen to survive and preserve competition in the marketplace; and we wouldn't have excessive executive compensation packages). However, the time it would take to complete these tasks would be problematic for our suitors from Consonance, who were expecting a more expeditious agreement.

On July 28, we got positive news from both the MIA and CMS. Ren Tundermann made a call to the insurance commissioner to sound him out on his timeline for having a deal in progress and was told that we would not be put into receivership on August 15, as long as the transaction was proceeding apace. Thank goodness for the continued support of Al Redmer.

Meanwhile, we talked to two of the professional finance staffers at CMS—Reed Cleary and Kevin Kendrick—to brief them on the deal we were hoping to bring to them for approval. I asked them explicitly if the conversion to for-profit status would be a deal breaker for CMS. The answer: as long as that was the only way that Evergreen could survive—and repay at least part of the original $65 million loan—the conversion should not be a problem.

Armed with this positive news, we reached out again to Consonance. They reviewed the new information, and we scheduled a conference call in which they would give us their decision. Since this was about the time we expected to hear the result of our appeal to the Fourth Circuit as well, the last few days of July were critical for Evergreen.

We also talked with the principals at Consonance in an effort to assuage their concern about another exorbitant risk adjustment assessment the next year. Even though the data we showed them demonstrated a very high probability of a risk adjustment assessment in the range of only $10 to $15 million the following year, on an estimated $175 million revenue base, the principals were not totally comfortable. So we had a second conference call with our actuaries from the Denver office of Milliman to put them more at ease. The Milliman actuaries made a very strong presentation, which went some of the way toward persuading Consonance, but the call ended without complete satisfaction for our potential investors. Nonetheless, seemingly reassured enough to proceed apace, Consonance agreed to meet with CMS for the initial presentation of our proposed transaction.

Since the court case, my wife had taken to sending me out the door with: "I hope nothing horrible happens at work today," instead of her usual, "Have a great day." On August 3, not five minutes went by before Manny Sheldon appeared at my office door, with a grim look on his face.

"Bad news—Columbia Bank has disapproved our bridge loan."

"I thought we had this guaranteed loan ready to go today!"

"The higher-ups in the bank went back on their pledge."

"What happened?"

"The bank is worried that the CO-OPs are all failing."

Well, this would certainly push one of them to the brink.

As we needed the guaranteed loan to bolster our reserves enough to keep us alive until a deal with our private equity partners was completed, this was a potentially fatal blow. To fill this void, our best bet now fell to getting the extra $6.5 million from Consonance as part of the deal.

While waiting to talk to Consonance, I held a staff meeting to bring our Evergreen team up to date. I took the group through the court cases, where we stood with the MIA, the transactions we were pursuing, and the possibility of being put into receivership by the MIA if things didn't work out. There were a lot of questions from the team, but *not one* was on the security of their jobs. To their great credit, virtually all their queries were about our ability to maintain our mission and keep control of the direction of the company, should we be converted to a for-profit. I know the same thing would never have happened at an all-staff meeting of one our competitors. In fact, the dedication to the value of their work was probably the greatest differentiator that Evergreen had, and it made me want to try even harder to keep the company going.

Unfortunately, that sentiment didn't seem to be enough. During our daily call with Consonance, Ben Edmands finally stated what I thought they had been thinking: the timeline we were all working on was simply too short to get a deal done by September 10, the risk adjustment payment due date (Redmer's new deadline). That would have been acceptable with a $6.5 million loan from Columbia Bank, which would have given us just enough reserves to bridge us to the completion of the deal with Consonance. But now, without that loan, our surplus would shrink to only a couple of million dollars the second that the $24 million payment went out the door.

That left us with only two options—find another bank that would be willing to give us a loan with the guarantees we had secured or find an investor(s) willing to fund a bridge loan and an actual acquisition. We had a couple of weeks to get a new loan before we had to book our assessment on August 15

(September 10 was the due date of the *payment*; the day we had to *book the assessment* of the payment amount was August 15, which, due to the unique rules of insurance accounting, would push our surplus below the legal limit on paper, allowing us to be put into receivership if the insurance commissioner so desired). Thus, we turned our efforts toward finding another bank willing to give us a loan.

Clearly, we were not a great risk, so approaching banks was a tricky proposition. Indeed, despite explaining that our efforts to ameliorate future risk adjustment payments would lead to us becoming an ongoing profitable entity, we found no takers among the dozen or more local and regional banks to whom we applied. This would lead us to pursue other potential lenders—who would want compensation at higher rates than the banks in return for taking on a risky loan.

Feeling anxious, I headed home, preparing mentally for our meeting the next day to discuss the proposed deal at CMS headquarters in Bethesda—even though we now had no actual investor or lender.

The next morning, August 4, while using the elliptical machine in our basement, I tuned the television to CNN. As it was 7 a.m., the morning news show was just coming on, with the first piece featuring dueling surrogates from the Trump and Clinton campaigns. To my surprise, one of the first criticisms of the current administration—and Hillary Clinton by extension—uttered by the Trump mouthpiece was that sixteen of the twenty-three CO-OPs had failed! We were now a talking point in the election season. The first thing I thought of was how we could use this as an argument if our meeting with CMS later that day didn't go well: "Does CMS really want attention brought to the CO-OP program if the most viable, profitable CO-OP was destroyed by CMS without repaying any of its federal loan?"

I met Burklund, Sheldon, and Sheldon's chief of staff, Bella Dieckmann, at the Starbucks across from the CO-OP program's headquarters in Bethesda about an hour before our meeting with CMS to go over our presentation. A smiling Sheldon and Dieckmann informed me that—shockingly—Consonance was not completely out of the picture after all. In fact, they gleefully showed me the arguments that Ben Edmands of Consonance had shared with them, which they were going to make to CMS via a conference call as part of our meeting.

Arriving at CMS, we were escorted upstairs to a cramped conference room by one of the professional financial staff members, Reed Cleary. Attending were Reed's colleague Kevin Kendrick, Jeff Wu, and Matt Lynch. Barely able to contain my disdain for the group that was largely responsible for putting us through immense and unnecessary stress, I remembered my wife's admonition that morning to channel my anger into productive use. In that vein, I presented everything that differentiated Evergreen from other CO-OPs and the rest of the marketplace, though occasionally throwing in a barb about the damage done by risk adjustment, and gave our arguments as to why conversion to a for-profit was good for Maryland. Ben Edmands did a great job giving commentary from Consonance's viewpoint. He was extremely supportive of Evergreen's model and philosophy of care and innovative practices, and he strongly criticized the entire risk adjustment process, stating that it gave them pause; and that they simply needed more time to complete due diligence.

Edmands then got off the phone so that we could present the terms of the deal that either Consonance or one of our other potential suitors would bring to CMS:

- CMS to push back repayment of startup loan by five years to allow for bridge financing, pending a conversion transaction
- Investor to buy out CMS loan at a discount to 5% (in other words, pay off 5% of our $62 million loan from the federal government)
- Investor to convert Evergreen Health to a for-profit entity
- Investor to bring PCOs into Evergreen Health by refinancing the $6M bank loan
- Investor to contribute additional capital to facilitate growth of enrollment to 100,000 members in five years
- CMS to waive 500% risk-based capital requirement and waive any actions against CO-OP as long as transaction is progressing, until conversion is finalized.

After our presentation, we awaited the CMS staffers' response. Amazingly, Lynch and his crew accepted a new deadline of mid- to late September for a term sheet on the deal, were fine with conversion to a for-profit, and didn't blink at our proposal to buy back the loan at five cents on the dollar. They agreed to take these terms to the Office of Management and Budget for quick review and said they'd get back to us in short order. Lynch closed the meeting by telling us that we were much further along on a deal and much more specific in our terms than any other CO-OP that had come to them with a proposal.

Sheldon and Burklund each rated the results of the meeting a 10 out of 10. I was not so sure, having been burned by CMS and the feds many times before. As Redmer texted me after I had briefed him on our meeting with CMS: "Great news—as long as they do what they say they're going to do." Dieckmann took notes and sent around the timeline and process that were agreed to in the meeting so that we could hold CMS to their word.

Driving back to Baltimore that evening, I was struck by how rapidly our fortunes had changed: we had gone from almost dead to potentially viable, in just eighteen hours!

Meanwhile, Al Redmer had requested a meeting with Evergreen's board of directors to let them know his thoughts on the current situation. The meeting with the MIA, on Tuesday, August 9, opened on a favorable note, with Redmer asking me to take his staff and our board through our current situation. I did that by drawing a timeline on our write-on wall: by August 15, with MIA's approval, we would have identified the still-unknown guarantors of a new \$6.5 million bridge loan (a loan to carry our finances at a level acceptable to the MIA until we obtained long-term funding from our eventual investors), to replace the one reneged on by Columbia Bank, which would take our RBC to just over 200%—just above the reserve level that could trigger an action by the MIA. With the bridge loan in place, we were to have a full term sheet (a firm description of all aspects of the conversion transaction) by mid- to late September, as agreed upon in our meeting with CMS, which would lead to our approval to move forward in 2017.

Al Redmer jumped in, by addressing the matter that had brought them to meet with our board. Should our potential deal(s) fall through, he wanted the board to vote to voluntarily agree to allow him to put us into receivership if we went below the minimum surplus level. By agreeing not to contest his action, we would buy ourselves a couple of additional weeks to finish our loan and get full term sheets from our private equity partners, before he would pull the trigger. If we didn't agree to voluntarily consent to receivership at his discretion, he would have to prepare the order to put us in receivership in the next few days or so, to allow time for a court to hear the case—which we all admitted would result in a verdict favoring the MIA's position. Although this was presented with tact by the commissioner, the Evergreen executive staff and the board came to a consensus to ask the commissioner if he could give Evergreen until its next board meeting to see what financing and/or deals we could obtain. If there was no real progress, the board would concede, and vote to voluntarily put us into receivership. Redmer agreed, and the board meeting adjourned.

Once again, Evergreen faced an existential threat—if we inked a deal and overcame the threat, Evergreen would go forward as a for-profit, mission-driven, innovative health insurer, with a strong private equity partner investing in the company's future success. If we didn't, at least the immensely stressful roller-coaster ride would be over.

In the early morning of August 10, several Evergreen sales staff and most of the executive team drove to the Eastern Shore of Maryland to speak to a large group of brokers in Easton, who served that section of the state. This was partly a reassurance visit (to let them know that we thought we would be fine, particularly after converting to a for-profit) and partly a rallying visit (to encourage them to sell our policies), since most of the Shore brokers were very upset with our competitor CareFirst's customer service and broker commission cuts. I found these direct meetings with our stakeholders particularly useful, as we got to hear their perspective on what we were doing right and what we were doing wrong. This group was no different; asking some tough questions, but giving us valuable information at the same time.

Unfortunately, upon returning from the Shore, Burklund broke the news that Consonance had decided to pass on the long-term financing/buyout deal. Apparently, as part of their vetting efforts, they gamed out our financial prospects should we suffer from enrollment attrition due to the continued public uncertainty of our viability, and they weren't confident we could survive.

Preparing for this possibility, I had reached out to Mark Puente for additional financing. Puente was a very well-connected healthcare leader who had served in a variety of public and private positions in the healthcare space in Maryland. I had interacted with him quite a lot in two of those capacities: as the deputy health secretary at the Maryland Department of Health and Mental Hygiene (when I was Baltimore City health commissioner), and as the CEO of Riverside Health—a Medicaid managed care organization (while I was at Evergreen). In fact, Puente was Evergreen's first board chair, a position he had to relinquish when our PCOs contracted with his Medicaid group to provide care to his patients as well as Evergreen's.

In the past few months, Puente's startup—Riverside—had been acquired by the University of Maryland Medical System and placed in a holding company, which housed Riverside and University Health Plan, a Medicare managed care company. The university system was intrigued by the possibility of acquiring us to round out their organization with a commercial insurer. Unlike the New York–based private equity firms, they were far more knowledgeable about the intricacies of the Maryland marketplace and the major players in the state. Thus, they would need much less time to do due diligence than would the out of state private equity firms.

Finally, the two companies that Puente ran (the Medicaid and Medicare entities) provided for economies of scale in terms of back-office activities. Puente's group had brought member services, claims, and billing, among others, in-house. Evergreen could save a substantial amount by piggybacking on those in-house services, rather than paying much higher rates for outsourced activities with poorly functioning third-party administrators. Clearly interested, Puente told us that he would talk to the University of Maryland Medical System's CFO the next day to sound him out on the idea of an acquisition of Evergreen.

Meanwhile, we pursued other avenues for financing. The most peculiar was a litigation financing loan, where we would be "fronted" a loan that would be paid back if we won the risk corridor litigation, resulting in significant receivables. (Although we had lost on the motion for a preliminary injunction, our federal lawsuit still awaited a full trial on its merits.) Several firms in New York offered such loans, and we were successful in obtaining $6 million from the Burford Group, which would loan us an additional $2 million if we needed it. Sheldon spent the day (August 12) walking on air, so thrilled was he with our current position. Although I was very happy to be back from the brink, I still wouldn't celebrate until the bridge loans had been signed, raising our surplus to a safe level.

I did fill Al Redmer, our insurance commissioner, in on recent developments, to which he replied in his inimitable fashion: "Great news! Keep up the good work! We are all rooting for you guys! Because . . . #1 . . . you are worth saving! and #2 . . . it will be a royal pain in my ass if you don't."

Then we learned of yet more changes in the requirements for our survival —this time from the MIA. In an email over the weekend and confirmed in a discussion with Redmer on August 29, we wouldn't be allowed to move forward on obtaining our bridge loans until we had proof of a buyout deal, which we had worked extremely hard to obtain in a timely manner, and now it wasn't enough.

Clearly, we wouldn't have a deal fully completed by September 10 (the date that the $24 million payment was due, which would leave us with less than $3 million in surplus—well below 90% RBC, and setting us up for receivership). We were now stuck: we weren't allowed to convert the bridge loans to reserves—which would keep us well above the actionable RBC level—until the buyout deal was under way. But the buyout deal wouldn't be able to happen before the payment deadline, which in itself would leave us with inadequate reserves.

The only solution to the conundrum was to see if CMS would give us an extension for our risk adjustment payment. This could occur in one of two ways: (a) a simple delay in the due date of the full amount; or (b) "netting" CMS payments due to us against our outstanding payment monthly (though not risk corridor receivables). In other words, CMS would withhold their monthly payments to Evergreen for the federal contribution to help cover premium payments for our members who were eligible for Obamacare subsidies (which amounted to about $3 million per month) until the $24 million we still owed was netted out. A call to Matt Lynch at CMS was in order.

Two days later, we received good news from Reed Cleary of CMS: with a deal in hand, CMS would not force us to send our entire risk adjustment payment on September 10. They would simply offset the various funds they owe us each month and subtract that amount from our risk adjustment payment.

Those of you closely following the ups and downs of our experience with CMS might say, "Hey, I thought that your lawsuit was asking to do exactly that with the risk corridor payments that CMS owed you!" And you'd be correct—this was yet another example of the inconsistent behavior of this agency (allowing offsetting of some types of revenue but not risk corridor).

By early September, after pursuing dozens of prospective investors following Consonance's declination, we finally had two very interested parties (NEWCO and Trusted Health) on the hook for both the acquisition deal and the additional $6.5 million in bridge loans (which, along with the $6 million in litigation financing from Burford, equaled the $12.5 million in bridge financing required by the MIA to keep Evergreen operating until the full deal had been completed). NEWCO was a consortium of regional investors;

Trusted Health was a Medicaid managed care organization operating out of Washington, DC. But before we could move forward with a deal, we needed CMS and MIA to let us know that they were okay with either group.

So, on Friday afternoon, September 2, with term sheets in hand, I called Al Redmer to review where we stood now. He agreed that the terms of the two loans didn't seem to have any significant problems. However, the MIA still held to the position that we couldn't draw down the loans to bolster our reserves until the application for conversion to a for-profit had formally been made by one of the investors. As both investor groups had a few more weeks of due diligence before they could commit to the deal, this meant that the loan proceeds would be delayed as well.

Technically speaking, since the $20-plus million we still owed on risk adjustment was gone from our books, we were currently insolvent, as we only had about $3 million in reserves (60% RBC). However, Redmer now assured us that if a deal was pending he wouldn't put us into receivership. Meanwhile, CMS was now taking a back seat in the process, leaving any potential action up to the MIA.

After delivering the term sheets to CMS, we now waited to see if the federal government would agree to write down our initial loan of $65 million to $3.25 million (our previously proposed five cents on the dollar) and allow us to be bought and converted to a for-profit.

I finally caught up with Lynch on September 9 to nail down final timetables, which changed again, but this time in our favor. The new requirements:

- OMB and CMS would provide us with written questions on the two potential bridge loans (NEWCO and Trusted Health) and their response to the two acquisition deal term sheets by the next Wednesday, September 14.
- We were to turn around our responses to the questions on the loans and the federal government's counterproposal (if there was one) on the cost to buy out CMS's loan ASAP.
- Assuming that there were still issues to discuss, a face-to-face meeting with CMS and OMB in Bethesda would be scheduled for the week of September 19 to work out the final terms of both the loans and the acquisition deal parameters.
- After coming to agreement on these issues, Evergreen would present the deal parameters to the two bidders and choose the winning

bidder by late September, giving the winning bidder time to prepare a final term sheet, including all the terms agreed to in our previous negotiations with CMS and OMB, and submit it to CMS, OMB, and MIA by September 30.

- This would allow time for final decision by CMS, OMB, and MIA by the October 15 deadline set by MIA for approving Evergreen to go on the Maryland Health Benefit Exchange to sell policies to individuals for 2017.

On September 12, we heard about a letter CMS had recently released. It was notification that CMS wouldn't have enough money in the risk corridor pot from 2015 to even cover the receivables owed for 2014. Not a surprising development, as this was long expected. What was not expected was delineated at the end of the letter:

> HHS recognizes that the Affordable Care Act requires the Secretary to make full payments to issuers. HHS will record risk corridors payments due as an obligation of the United States Government for which full payment is required.
>
> We know that a number of issuers have sued in federal court seeking to obtain the risk corridors amounts that have not been paid to date. As in any lawsuit, the Department of Justice is vigorously defending those claims on behalf of the United States. However, as in all cases where there is litigation risk, we are open to discussing resolution of those claims. We are willing to begin such discussions at any time.

Amazingly, HHS was stating what we had set forth in our lawsuit. I was incredulous (I would have been apoplectic if I hadn't become somewhat inured to CMS's actions). If this letter had been released just a few weeks earlier, there was no question in my mind that Judge Russell would have ruled for us on the claim that we should be allowed to offset our risk adjustment payment with the $20-plus million in risk corridor payments we were owed by CMS.

The following morning, I watched as CMS's acting administrator, Andy Slavitt, was grilled by the House Energy and Commerce Committee during a hearing on the ACA and CO-OPs. At one point, a Republican congressman from Virginia, Morgan Griffith, having obviously heard rumblings about the possibility of risk corridor payments being made, asked Slavitt if he intended to make risk corridor payments to carriers in amounts greater than those allowed by Congress. (Remember, the GOP had passed an amendment stating that risk corridor payments to carriers with a loss had to equal risk corridor payments made to the carriers that were making money. The disparity between losers and winners was 8:1, resulting in risk corridor payments that were only one-eighth of those expected.) Slavitt answered affirmatively. Taken aback, the Virginia lawmaker asked if CMS's counsel was talking to the Department of Justice about making risk corridor payments from a separate source—the little-known federal Judgment Fund. Slavitt noted that that was a question for the lawyers, but pointedly didn't deny it.

Watching this and thinking a bit more about HHS's remarkable memo, it instantly became clear: by literally asking—no, encouraging—carriers to sue over risk corridor payments due to them, and offering to settle—the US Department of Health and Human Services was effectively doing an end-run around the Republican congressional action limiting risk corridor funding to a budget-neutral pool. HHS was instead intending to use the Judgment Fund, over which the Congress had very limited authority, to pay any settlements. Although too late for seventeen CO-OPs and many other former carriers, this potentially helpful suggestion by Slavitt might offer us a lifeline by securing the risk corridor funds we were due.

I was immediately on the phone with Caroline Brown about our filing a suit going after our risk corridor receivables as soon as possible. We couldn't sue the federal government on similar grounds in separate federal courts, so the plan was to sever the claim of our original case immediately (although we hadn't been granted a preliminary injunction, our original federal lawsuit was still in play), and then launch a new suit in federal claims court for the $23-plus million in risk corridor payments we were owed for the past two years.

Just when we thought we had heard it all, on Thursday, September 15, another gut punch got thrown at us, this time by the OMB. Our buyout deal term sheets had been submitted to CMS at the beginning of the month and then sent along to OMB for their approval on the buyout of the federal loan. Now Matt Lynch of CMS was the bearer of bizarre bad news. OMB approved buying out our $65 million loan at five cents on the dollar. However, based on Slavitt's recent pronouncement about CMS's apparent intention to make risk corridor payments owed to various carriers, OMB now insisted on adding 100% of risk corridor payments owed to us from 2014, 2015, and 2016 to our overall value. Thus, to acquire us, an entity would have to pay $3.25 million (for the buyout of CMS's loan) and pay off our $12.5 million bridge loans, and now an additional $34 million (the estimate for our *three years* of receivables from risk corridor), making the entire transaction over $30 million more than had been anticipated. Neither of our potential buyers would even remotely consider continuing negotiations with us for a deal that would be almost three times costlier than they had expected, especially given the lack of certainty that risk corridor would ever be paid—despite Slavitt's recent pronouncements.

The only other option, according to Lynch, was to give up our rights to ever receive any risk corridor payments owed to Evergreen. This would not have been of much concern to potential buyers as recently as the previous week, when no one expected the feds to ever pay much of the risk corridor receivables owed to carriers around the country. However, with the recent CMS statement and Andy Slavitt's congressional testimony, it had become clear that risk corridor payments were now more likely to be made. Therefore, a prospective buyer would have to give up the potential for $30-plus million in risk corridor payments down the road under this second option.

One further possibility that occurred to me was that if the feds considered our risk corridor receivables an obligation for the federal government, then we should be able to book it as an asset. Doing so would immediately make us profitable, giving us a 500% RBC level. We wouldn't even need to convert to a for-profit, though a buyout deal from CMS sooner rather than later would be tremendously better than remaining under the thumb of this capricious agency. But of course, this was not to be.

After digesting this news, I called Redmer to fill him in and get his counsel. He said that if he were the buyer, giving up the risk corridor payments wouldn't bother him much because the track record of CMS was not exactly stellar in terms of delivering on their promises. He thought the deal on its face was sweet enough without risk corridor. The only problem with this approach was that we would still need the $12.5 million in bridge loans, but by signing away our rights to any risk corridor receivables, we would have eliminated the Burford litigation financing loan. This would require us to obtain $6 million to offset the loss of the Burford loan in the next couple of weeks. So off we went to search for another lender.

Yet another bizarre twist in CMS's position on risk corridor came to light in mid-September, through a discussion with one of our lawyers, Phil Peisch.

In a talk with an attorney at the Department of Justice, Peisch found out that DOJ had not preapproved the CMS letter encouraging settlement of risk corridor claims, but DOJ was about to start negotiations on a settlement of an anticipated class action by all claimants to risk corridor payments. Again, that settlement would most assuredly come from the Judgment Fund, over which Congress had little control. The Republicans in Congress, under the signature of Energy and Commerce Committee chair Fred Upton, having gotten wind of this the week before, immediately issued a missive to HHS Secretary Burwell, which in part said:

> Due to this [risk corridor] shortfall, several insurance companies have filed lawsuits against the federal government, requesting that CMS pay insurers the full amount requested. On Friday, September 9, 2016, CMS published a memorandum regarding the insurers' lawsuits . . . express[ing] CMS' willingness to settle the lawsuits with the insurance companies although the U.S. Department of Justice (DOJ)—CMS's attorneys in the cases—has argued that the suits are not ripe for consideration. . . .
>
> . . . Since Congress acted twice to protect taxpayer dollars by prohibiting the use of federal funds to make up for any shortfall in risk corridors payments, the Committee is concerned about the Administration's intent to use any federal funds to settle the suits brought by the insurance companies. It appears that any such settlements would come from the permanent appropriations for judgments ("Judgment Fund"). . . .
>
> . . . Further, the Administration's explicit offer to settle these lawsuits appears to be a direct circumvention of the clear Congressional intent to prohibit the expenditure of federal dollars on this program.

While waiting to see what came of this new CMS move, on September 28, we scrambled to get the term sheets for the guaranteed bridge loan and the acquisition transaction ready to go to CMS. By 4:15 p.m., all term sheets were in hand, and I sent an email to our friends at CMS and the MIA: "Please find attached three term sheets: (a) term sheet for guaranteed bridge loan from Sports Capital Lending [NEWCO] (signed copy to be forwarded), (b) term sheet for conversion transaction from NEWCO, (c) term sheet for conversion transaction from Trusted Health. Please note that our Board of Directors will be making the decision on which group we will go forward with to convert Evergreen to a for-profit insurer at a special meeting on Monday, October 3,

2016." Lynch replied that he would get the review process going with OMB and would keep us updated. With that, we awaited CMS, OMB, and MIA's decisions on whether we were good to go to sell on the Maryland exchange on November 1, and continue selling group policies throughout 2017.

The *Washington Post's* Amy Goldstein—a well-regarded health reporter—had recently talked with me about the pending deal and was ready to go with the story as soon as she could report on the Evergreen Board of Directors' vote. Within an hour of the board's adjournment, an article with the following headline was on the *Post's* website: "Maryland's ACA health co-op will switch to for-profit to save itself." Shortly thereafter, the *Baltimore Sun* announced: "Evergreen Health to be acquired, convert to for-profit insurance company." These pieces were beneficial to Evergreen, because they would let the marketplace know that we were viable and safe to place business with for the upcoming sales season.

The night closed on a nice note with this lovely, supportive email from one of our members (whom I knew through our children's school):

Dear Peter,

I am thinking of you today.

I became an Evergreen member 1/1/2016. I LOVE Evergreen. In all my years from disability & medical underwriter, through human capital management consultant, to startup entrepreneur, to mom who buys the family health plan, I want you to know, Evergreen's model and healthcare operations are hands-down, the best approach I have ever seen or encountered. I tell everyone I know about my first physical with Evergreen (Dr. DeLong) and what a delightful and surprising experience it was. When I didn't have time to set a few appointments for referrals she provided, I received a friendly call that nudged me to make my preventive care appointment and I felt good that Evergreen was watching out for me.

I am relieved Evergreen will live to fight another day.

A nice reminder of why we'd created Evergreen.

In early October, the Evergreen Board of Directors voted to choose NEWCO as the investor to go forward with our deal. By this time, with Redmer's optimism that a deal would eventually get done, the MIA had lowered the amount of financing we needed to keep going to $8 million from $12.5 million. Shortly thereafter, one of the principals of the NEWCO investor group (which was now the financier of the guaranteed $8 million loan) came to our headquarters to meet with two of the individuals—Mark Puente and Chris Brandt—

who were now interested in participating in the loan guarantee in return for an equity stake in Evergreen when the conversion/acquisition transaction closed. What we thought would be a simple agreement on the terms of the guarantee rapidly spun out of control when the potential guarantors' lawyer started pressing the NEWCO representative for concessions (namely, some monetary upside for guaranteeing the loan). With Manny Sheldon sitting to my right, providing commentary on the rapidly changing terms, it became clear to me that we wouldn't have the signed letters from the guarantors affirming their intentions that we had promised the MIA by the end of the day.

The next day, October 7, started with an early morning email from Redmer laying out the MIA's case that we had insufficient reserves to go on as a viable insurer. Their math showed that our reserves were a negative $4 million. The MIA accountants, even with the $8 million guaranteed loan, argued that we would only have reserves of $4 million, or 74% RBC, until the deal closed. Per the MIA counsel, Van Dorsey, we should be placed into receivership or be liquidated. With this development, I was sure that Redmer would finally pull the plug on Evergreen when we went to meet him later that week at the MIA offices in downtown Baltimore.

Upon entering the room, I felt that my supposition was correct, as Redmer flipped over his notepad as if to conceal his pronouncement, and ten MIA staffers filed in quietly. I provided evidence of the interest and commitment of the buyers to do the deal. All NEWCO needed was a little more time beyond October 31 to complete their financial vetting of Evergreen. The meeting ended with an agreement that the MIA would remain patient if CMS didn't push the matter. Redmer did pull me aside to talk briefly about the calculations of his staff showing our inadequate reserves; I replied that we didn't agree with some of their statements and that we would address them with the accountants over the next couple of weeks.

Walking out of the meeting, I marveled that we had not only averted immediate shutdown but had seemingly bought weeks more to finalize both the bridge loan and the overall transaction.

That is, until two hours later, while I was having coffee with my parents, I received a call from Al Redmer. Lynch had just informed him that if Evergreen didn't go on the individual exchange, CMS would not allow us to go forward at all, and we now had only one week—until the following Friday, October 14—to have the investors show they had "skin in the game" in the form of putting up some of the guarantees for the loan. Again, a completely unexpected new requirement was being imposed by CMS. So, to the phone Burklund and I went—me to the individual Baltimore-area investors, and Burklund to inform the representative of both potential investor groups, NEWCO and Trusted Health, of the new deadline, with a plan to meet with CMS in the coming week just as we had done with the MIA.

Five hours later, I got another late Friday email from Lynch—which never boded well. Yet another ultimatum had come from the bureaucrats of CMS, contradicting what Redmer had told us just hours earlier. In it, Lynch relayed several last-minute changes in CMS's conditions for the deal to be completed. Perhaps most exasperating was the requirement that our investors produce a signed "back-out fee," the funds from which would go toward covering the future medical claims of our membership in the event of a wind-down should the investors back out.

To make matters worse, CMS gave us one business day to meet all their requests. Since their continual rule changes had created the need for new agreements to be developed, their asking for a back-out fee was laughable. In return, I should have asked for a back-out fee from CMS to reimburse us for our efforts to re-create all aspects of our deal, just because of CMS's repeated arbitrary and unexpected deviations from the rules.

We requested an immediate meeting with CMS for our investors to turn their fire on the bureaucrats to try to buy a little more time. Ironically, a superb editorial came out the same day in the *Baltimore Sun*, heaping praise on Evergreen's model and contribution to Maryland, while urging us to keep to our mission as we became a for-profit enterprise. It complimented our philosophy of aligning an insurance company with innovative primary care offices and our use of evidence-based practices and concluded with a strong endorsement of the need to keep a local, pioneering health carrier in Maryland's health insurance marketplace, to keep costs lower for all Marylanders.

As of Sunday, October 9, here's where things stood:

1. Our board of directors had selected the investor group—NEWCO.
2. We had the terms of the acquisition deal:
    - $3.275 million for buying out the CMS loan
    - $8 million in guarantees on a bridge loan to maintain adequate surplus until the deal closed

- $5 million in cash to increase our reserves, when the deal closed
- $1.5 million in deal expenses
- For a total of $17.775 million.

3. MIA required us to have signed letters from all guarantors for the $8 million loan by Friday, October 14; MIA would allow us to go forward with this $8 million through the deal closure (with a possible requirement of $2 million additional cash at end of year).

4. CMS required us to have the same by Tuesday, October 11. They also wanted a back-out fee paid by the investors (which we wouldn't agree to).

5. If the above deadlines were met, CMS and MIA would approve us to sell policies on Maryland's individual Obamacare exchange starting November 1, 2016, and to sell all policies throughout 2017.

If all above deadlines were met, a full application for acquisition of Evergreen and its conversion to a for-profit would be delivered to Maryland Insurance Commissioner Al Redmer in November. A public hearing would follow, after which the commissioner would presumably approve the deal, starting a ninety-day waiting period, which would conclude with the deal closing in February 2017.

Chapter Ten

Staying Alive

October 2016

Facing a CMS-imposed October 11 deadline to produce the guarantors of the $8 million bridge loan, we spent the next couple of days frantically chasing down the various potential loan participants.

Our local colleague, Mark Puente, had come through big time. With his consortium of several colleagues, the Puente group raised $4 million of the bridge loan (which would be converted to capital should the consortium take eventual ownership of Evergreen). One of his co-investors was Scott Rifkin, a successful entrepreneurial physician I had stayed friendly with over the past thirty years, since he and I shared an on-call room during medical residency. We still needed an additional $4 million, which Al Redmer had intimated should come from the new investors, to show they had skin in the game.

However, multiple calls among the parties and ourselves left Jonathan Burklund quite pessimistic about the NEWCO investors' willingness to sign a guarantee—at least for now. I called one of the principals of NEWCO to inform him of the absolute deadline imposed by the Maryland Insurance Administration (the end of the week), should we get past the CMS Tuesday deadline. He was convinced that he could "charm" CMS and MIA to push the deadline back. He argued that the CMS staff were political animals and wouldn't want a CO-OP failing less than four weeks before the presidential election. I felt that CMS couldn't care less, but we ended the call with the principal assuring me that he could move the deadline by two weeks.

After a couple of calls with Puente and Chris Brandt in which they reassured me of their willingness to participate in the bridge loan, we agreed to reconnoiter shortly after the Puente/Brandt/Rifkin group had conferenced with their consortium of new investors.

First thing the following morning, Manny Sheldon, Burklund, and I regrouped to discuss our options should NEWCO not put up the other $4 million in guarantees. We went back to Burford for another run at a litigation financing loan. They were willing to put up a $4 million loan in return for about double that amount of potential risk corridor payments down the road. With the $8 million in guarantees now in hand, I set up an urgent meeting with Matt Lynch, urging him not to act against us until we could talk.

We had the conversation with Lynch mid-morning of October 11, during which he made it crystal clear that we had to get the signed commitments for the bridge loan to CMS that same day, and CMS/OMB wanted a back-out fee as part of the overall deal. That day's deadline was necessary because the Office of Management and Budget needed at least a couple of days to analyze the loans and approve the overall deal (in order to have us approved to go on the Obamacare exchange for open enrollment). According to Lynch, there was simply no wiggle room. Worried that we might be shut down by the end of the day, I called Redmer to get his take. He confirmed his earlier deadline of the upcoming Friday, the 14th, for the signed commitments for the $8 million in loans.

When assured that $4 million of it would come from the investors (Puente, Brandt, and Rifkin were now co-investors, since their loans would eventually be converted to equity), the commissioner was comfortable that the investors now had enough on the table to negate the need for an additional back-out fee.

We then had a follow-up call with several CMS staff, including Matt Lynch, along with NEWCO's representative. This was NEWCO's attempt to push back at CMS—and he did a good job of it. After I told Lynch of my exchange with Redmer and his satisfaction with our plan, the NEWCO principal weighed in to ask why October 11 was a deadline at all. Lynch quickly backed down, and by the end of the call we didn't owe anything to CMS for ten more days!

However, on that same call, we were shocked to hear the NEWCO representative tell the CMS staff that there was a good chance that the whole $8 million would be put up by a billion-dollar health system! Where did that come from? As soon as we got off the phone with Lynch with the understanding that we had until October 21 to get CMS the committed loan documents, we took a call from the NEWCO partner. "With all due respect," I said, "what are you talking about in terms of this health system?" Coyly, he declined to say, indicating that he would be in hot water if he disclosed this information until later in the week. I told him that he should be aware that a conversion deal required evaluations of the deal's antitrust ramifications and community interest consequences—both of which might well be affected if a large health system were involved.

He promised to identify the entity shortly, and we concluded the call with a plan that we would get signed commitments from the Puente/Brandt/Rifkin group and the Burford group for their respective loans to MIA by the Friday the 14th deadline, and if NEWCO could structure a deal with all needed monies to come from this mysterious health system by CMS's deadline ten days hence, we could simply cancel the other guarantees.

Then, in another unexpected twist, with arrangements still fluid, the Puente group abruptly notified us that if they put in half of the bridge loan funds, they didn't want to participate in a deal with NEWCO at all. In fact, they would raise the funds to buy us and convert us to a for-profit themselves. In other words, the Puente Group was no longer interested in being part of a deal with NEWCO or any affiliate. The Puente Group would control the deal.

We had long harbored reservations about the opaque NEWCO group's ability to complete the whole deal. Thus, with a group well known to us (and the MIA) openly showing us the money, we decided that we would need to get out of our deal with NEWCO. The responsibility for making the call to the NEWCO principal fell to Manny, who had the best relationship with him. Meanwhile, we worked feverishly to get commitment letters for the bridge loan from Burford and the Puente Group to send to the MIA in time to meet their deadline.

We spent the morning with the attorneys for the Puente Group, now known as JARS (mostly an acronym made up of the first letter of the last names of some of the individual investors). After finally getting to an agreement with JARS, we locked up Burford's loan commitment as well.

Meanwhile, we had two very uncomfortable calls with the principals of NEWCO to inform them that, since they had not come through with any funding or put together a viable consortium, while JARS had done so, we had to acquiesce to JARS's demand to control the deal. NEWCO was not happy, as we had had an exclusive with them, but we reminded them of the unpleasant surprise that NEWCO had unleashed on us during our CMS call Tuesday, that they were shopping us to a hospital system—a clear violation of our deal that they couldn't disclose any of our proprietary information without our approval.

Late that night Ren Tundermann, our regulatory attorney, sent me an email that reinforced our concerns about the NEWCO investor group, in which she noted that the principal of NEWCO had really offended Lynch in their call earlier that week, and Lynch had passed along his dissatisfaction to Redmer.

Amazingly, I received a call the next morning, October 14, from that very same NEWCO principal, asking my permission for him to call Tori Bayless, the CEO of Anne Arundel Health System (AAHS)—the mysterious hospital he had referred to in Tuesday's call with Lynch. Apparently, NEWCO had been talking with Bayless, and Anne Arundel was now interested in being part of the acquisition. As we were now less than two hours from Commissioner Redmer's meeting with Puente—and NEWCO had not delivered on any of their promises for weeks—I wrote back to NEWCO to cease and desist. I also called Bayless to tell her that it was too late for any additional immediate deals. We did not want to do anything to confuse the situation for the MIA at this point, as a decision was imminent.

Conceivably, if the commissioner approved the bridge loans from JARS and Burford Capital to keep us going, the JARS group could come back to AAHS on their own for some further capital that they would need to complete the final acquisition (which is exactly what happened soon thereafter).

We waited impatiently for the results of the meeting at the MIA. Finally, Tundermann called us to give the summary of their discussion. First, the MIA had a negative opinion of the NEWCO group and was not satisfied that they would complete the deal. Second, the MIA and Redmer were pleased with the composition of JARS—Redmer knew the individuals personally and was very comfortable with them. Third, his staff was not terribly comfortable with the Burford litigation finance loan. So, we had two options to be certified for the exchange:

1. JARS could turn in a signed commitment for a $4 million loan, with that loan to be funded by the next Friday, the 21st; *and* $4 million

more in loans would be funded by October 26; *and* commitments
for an additional $3 to $7 million to get our surplus above 200%
risk-based capital must be obtained by December 31. (This was the
commissioner's preferred option.)
or

2. JARS could turn in the signed commitment later for the $4 million
   loan; *and* we could turn in a signed agreement for the Burford Group's
   $4 million loan.

The commissioner made it clear that he could revoke our certification to sell
on the individual exchange at any time if he lost confidence in the ultimate
acquisition deal with the JARS group closing in a timely fashion.

By the end of the day, Puente's negotiation efforts seemed to have borne
fruit, as AAHS (yes, they were now inside on the deal) had agreed to cover
the additional $4 million to substitute for Burford Capital's much costlier
loan. With $8 million now committed, which would guarantee us entry onto
the individual exchange and solidify our path to survival, you would think it
would be a time to celebrate. However, in inimitable Evergreen fashion, there
was a fly in the ointment—this time self-imposed.

It seems that Manny, in his haste to nail down the abstruse NEWCO group,
had gotten too far over his skis. The agreement he made with NEWCO had
not been adequately vetted by our attorneys and was not as protective of us
as it should have been. Now, as part of the deal with JARS, we had to certify
that we were completely out of any arrangement with another investor group.
We thought that Al Redmer's discomfort with the NEWCO group's proposal
served to unlink us from them, but that apparently wasn't accurate. What
followed was a frenzied negotiation with NEWCO, which wanted tens of
thousands of dollars for a breakup fee. Meanwhile, we were taking incoming
heat from JARS's attorney and from our own regulatory counsel, Ren Tundermann, for not clearing things with them first. It was evident, after a few contentious calls, that nerves were fraying, and some longstanding antagonisms
between some of the players were coming to a head.

Having become more judicious over time, I implored everyone to take a
deep breath and remember how far we had come and just to work together to
get to the finish line. So, after Tundermann drafted a strong termination letter to NEWCO, and Burklund negotiated a monetary settlement of $125,000,

we extricated ourselves from the NEWCO group and were free to enter into an agreement with JARS.

We now turned our sights to obtaining funds from the newest member of our investor group—Anne Arundel Health Systems. AAHS was the parent company of the Anne Arundel Medical Center (AAMC), a well-regarded regional medical complex, located in Annapolis, the state capital. Having worked with AAHS and much of their executive staff in relation to our collaboration with them as one of Evergreen's preferred providers, we looked forward to working with them on this new joint effort.

To that end, the AAHS executive team came to meet with our senior leadership team at Evergreen for a full briefing. We thought the purpose of this meeting was to provide additional comfort to those on the team who had not met with us previously. However, it soon became clear that they weren't here only to get comfortable with the deal; they were questioning us in a way that implied that they had not made any concrete decisions about contributing to the bridge loan or the full acquisition. This contradicted Puente and his attorney's assurances that AAHS was committed to joining forces with JARS for the loan and the acquisition transactions. Some of the AAHS team didn't even understand the importance of their $4 million contribution to the bridge loan, with one of their executives asking what would happen if AAHS didn't provide the $4 million (to which I replied that we would close as of Friday).

After the meeting, Manny, Burklund, Roberta Hurst, and I retreated to Manny's office to debrief. Could this be the case—that AAHS might not be in? Especially after we had jettisoned our two other possible lifelines—Burford and NEWCO—at the request of JARS? While we were talking, Burklund was pulled out of the room by JARS's lawyer, George Nemphos. His good news was that our presentation this morning had impressed the AAHS executives and didn't raise any red flags. The bad news was that AAHS indeed wasn't solid on the deal. And, if they did do the deal, they were insisting on a majority position, even if the contributions were evenly split between AAHS and JARS. Nemphos told them to go pound sand, and gave Burklund 30–70 odds against a deal being completed between the two groups by Friday, when an $8 million loan had to be funded, per Al Redmer.

Of further concern, AAHS went radio-silent on JARS for much of the day, leading Nemphos to ask me to reach out to them. Things calmed down a bit when Puente called me later to say that he had finally been in touch with

AAHS executives, who had two requests before going to their board for a final vote on Wednesday afternoon: (a) confirmation from CMS that they would take five cents on the dollar to buy out the CMS loan (I had asked Reed Cleary at CMS to request such a confirmation, which he promised by the next morning); and (b) reassurance from Al Redmer that all that was required on Friday was $8 million in loans from AAHS and JARS, with a further commitment to complete the deal down the road.

With this information, all parties took a deep breath—the deal appeared to be on track again.

That is, until later that evening, when I checked my email one more time before bed and found a message from Matt Lynch, throwing yet another wrench into the plan. In direct contradiction to assurances given to me just days earlier by his own staff, that CMS would confirm the terms of the deal, Lynch said he would do nothing of the sort. Moreover, he told me that we were under extreme time constraints for approval of our deal before open enrollment began in a week's time. And I wasn't to forget that the start of open enrollment was CMS's newly imposed deadline for us to get federal consent for the deal.

I replied that the terms of the new deal were simple, and known to all parties: $3.275 million to pay off the CMS loan, $8 million for the bridge loan, $7 million committed to increase the bridge loan until closing if RBC was inadequate, and $1.4 million closing costs. Furthermore, in return for five cents on the dollar, we were to waive all risk corridor receivables (except the $2.5 million on our books), and convert to a for-profit entity via Maryland law conversion process. I said we needed confirmation before the next afternoon.

First thing on October 19, I made several calls to Lynch to try to reason with him that the new bridge loan / acquisition terms were almost identical to those they had already seen, and the OMB had given their blessing to the five cents on the dollar buyout of the CMS loan. Not receiving a call back, I phoned Redmer, who called Lynch. The result: CMS would not budge.

The constant slippage of deadlines and threatened shutdowns had become a running joke on my nightly calls with my parents. Despite my protestations that "such and such a date was a hard stop, really," my dad would pooh-pooh my claims and would invariably be correct.

So now we were on the hunt to get AAHS board approval of the bridge loan and the acquisition term sheets. Fortunately, Redmer was able to convince their board to support the deal.

Within minutes of receiving the term sheets, I signed for Evergreen, and the sheets were immediately sent to the MIA and CMS for their approval. The only condition of the proposed deal that I was concerned about in terms of approval from the feds and the state was the requirement by the investors that due diligence be extended through December 31. This would mean the deal would likely not close until April or May 2017, leaving an awful lot of time for potential issues to arise and destroy it (as Tundermann, our superb outside counsel, said at the time, "time is the enemy of any deal"). But they insisted, and so the sheets were in the hands of our regulators awaiting their decision.

As we expected, the MIA expressed no qualms. By Friday the 21st, Tundermann told me that we were in good shape—both AAHS and JARS were on board, and Redmer would quickly approve the term sheets as soon as he got them and would push CMS for rapid agreement, as well.

Redmer then called Lynch to get CMS's read. About 3:45 p.m., I texted Redmer: "Any news?" He replied that the call went well and that he had assured Matt Lynch that the MIA was comfortable with the deal, which reassured Lynch. Redmer then noted that he would follow up with CMS and was hopeful that he could allow the funding of the loan at the beginning of the next week.

The term sheets were sent to CMS and MIA before 5 p.m., and I closed out the week with the following upbeat but not conclusive (I had learned my lesson not to assume any outcome until it actually occurred) email to our Evergreen board:

> Dear Board—Good news to end the week . . . MIA is supportive of our $8 million loan term sheet as well as the acquisition term sheet. In a discussion today with the CO-OP team at CMS, Commissioner Redmer reported that they did not raise any opposition to any of the terms in the agreements but are running it up the flagpole at CMS/OMB and will have a final decision for us by Wednesday. If the decision is positive, the $8 million loan will fund on Wednesday, immediately boosting our surplus above 100% RBC. We may not need any additional funds until closing of the acquisition (but the lenders are willing to do so if necessary). As it turned out, in a last minute frenzy of activity, the groups that put up the loan will also be acquiring Evergreen. The groups involved in both transactions switched up as well in the last few days—the investors going forward are Anne Arundel Health Systems and JARS Group (composed of four individual investors from Baltimore with extensive health system experience).

Bottom line: as long as the loans fund by Wednesday we will be allowed on the exchange and to sell group plans in 2017 and beyond—in other words, we will be a going concern.

Big thanks also to Ren Tundermann for her excellent work as counsel for the deal and VERY SPECIAL THANKS TO INSURANCE COMMISSIONER AL REDMER, who has been incredibly supportive throughout this torturous process.

I knew something bad had happened when I returned from coaching Hank's soccer team at 10:30 on Saturday morning, October 22, to find four messages from Redmer and Tundermann, and an email from Matt Lynch requesting a call. Checking first with Redmer, I learned that Lynch had called him to say that CMS had decided there wasn't enough time to evaluate our term sheets and approve them for us to go on the exchange.

Lynch reached me shortly thereafter and gave me even more dire news: CMS, in consultation with other federal agencies, had determined that time had run out and that they weren't going to approve the deal, period. I demanded that Lynch tell me who had made the decision. After hemming and hawing, he eventually told me what I suspected—Andy Slavitt. I pointed out that we had done our part—we had delivered a complete deal to them back in early September, when OMB had approved our buyout of the CMS loan at five cents on the dollar, but CMS had changed the game on September 15, by forcing us to account for risk corridor receivables, destroying the deal. Lynch agreed that this was true. We had then worked tirelessly to come up with another, better deal in only four weeks (when most such acquisition deals take six to nine months to be developed), which MIA had already approved with one day's notice. How could they not be able to turn around a decision on a deal similar to, though simpler than, the one presented to them just one month earlier?

Lynch just kept muttering that he was sorry. "So, this is it, then," I asked— "CMS would not approve the deal at all, correct? This shuts us down Monday then." No comment from Lynch.

Now trying for a couple of Hail Marys, I called Senator Cardin's chief of staff, Chris Lynch (no relation to Matt), to see if the senator could pressure Slavitt. I was surprised to hear that Chris already knew we would be shut down, because Slavitt had called Cardin the previous evening to inform him of this decision. According to Chris, the senator was "spitting mad" and lambasted Slavitt mercilessly, to the point where the senator had told Chris that he hoped Slavitt might reconsider. Apparently not.

I then called the #2 official at CMS, Kevin Counihan, who rarely returned my calls. Surprisingly he did call back, and I unleashed a scathing invective against his agency's actions. For nearly ten minutes, I went through the litany of obstacles they had raised that we had overcome—from changed deadlines to altered rules—with such forcefulness that I scared my two sons, who were in the car with me at the time.

Although he claimed that the information and timeline I was providing him was news to him (though I highly doubted it), he bent a little and asked me to put all my arguments into a paper for Slavitt and him to review that evening.

For the next two hours I put together a summary of how we had met every changing deadline and followed all CMS guidelines, a process that had culminated with a solid deal, strongly approved by our state regulator, Al Redmer. I sent the memo to Counihan and Slavitt by 8:30 p.m.

Counihan texted me Sunday night to tell me that a decision would be forthcoming by early morning at the latest. Not able to sleep past five, I went into the office at six on Monday, October 24, to anxiously await news of our fate. Apparently, CMS had been working on our case since my memo of Saturday night. At nine, Counihan called back to let me know that CMS was meeting with "very senior" HHS officials at eleven. As 2:30 came around, Counihan finally called me: "Not good news: we can't approve the deal." The reason, he said, was that "we've seen sixteen of these deals before [what was he talking about?], and they never go the way you say they will. It isn't the timing, it's the plan, the money is not sufficient, and we don't think the investors will complete the deal. Also, the deal goes on too long. May is too late for it to close, so, we can't approve it."

And just like that, Evergreen again appeared to be dead. The most successful and most innovative CO-OP launched by the Affordable Care Act had been knowingly done in by the agency ostensibly responsible for its success.

Stunned, I called Redmer to learn about the receivership process. Our board would be asked to consent to putting us into receivership in the next couple of days, which would be followed with a court filing to do so. We would, of course, be decertified from selling on the exchange on November 1 and would have to cease selling all new policies immediately.

A receiver would show up at our door within a week and would meet with me before taking over the company. Which employees would stay and which would be forced to leave would be up to the receiver—obviously, sales and marketing staff would be the first to go. However, we were likely to keep some operations going (like billing and customer service) as far as the end of the next year, since policies in effect would continue until they termed at the end of twelve months, although the number of enrollees would tail off quickly.

After that uplifting conversation, I entertained some last-gasp suggestions. First, from Burklund and Manny: What if we raised $4 million more from our investors, to raise us over 200% of RBC? I called Counihan to propose that tack. "Give me thirty minutes," he said. Thirty minutes later, Counihan called back: "No go, we need $24 million at a minimum." Twenty-four million dollars? Redmer had accepted $8 million, but now we needed more than triple that! Clearly, CMS didn't want us to survive.

Chapter Eleven

Riding a Roller Coaster

October 2016 to January 2017

In response to CMS's denial of our deal, a suggestion came from Ren Tunder-mann. Have the investors put up an additional $3.275 million in cash to repay the CMS loan at five cents on the dollar (which had already been approved by OMB for the deal in September). As part of the agreement we would then waive our rights to any risk corridor receivables we were owed. We would then amend our charter and remove our status as a cooperative. Finally, the investors would put up the $8 million in reserves already approved by the Maryland Insurance Administration and move forward with the conversion to a for-profit.

Sounds familiar, doesn't it? Well, we had proposed just such a solution to CMS multiple times in the past and were rejected each time. Feeling whip-sawed, I was a bit reluctant to call Kevin Counihan with another Hail Mary, but I went ahead. Counihan sounded slightly interested and asked me to give him until tomorrow to get back to me. Not trusting him for a second, I held out little hope of a last-minute reprieve and went to sleep.

Waking to news shows and the *New York Times* alike highlighting skyrock-eting Obamacare premiums only two weeks before the election, I figured I'd take one more stab at referencing the political damage CMS's decision was likely to inflict on the administration and by extension on Hillary Clinton's campaign. I sent a strong email to Andy Slavitt and Counihan shortly after 8 a.m., on Tuesday, October 25, which made the following points:

> Considering the fact that the huge increases in Obamacare premiums are clearly going to be one of the paramount issues in the two weeks leading up to the election, I would think President Obama would prefer not to have the story of how the leaders of his own agency responsible for implementation of the ACA killed the most successful and innovative CO-OP.
>
> Put aside, for now, the immensely deleterious effects of CMS's absolute refusal to consider any reasonable risk adjustment remediation options, any of which would have preserved many of the new market entrants that went down because of the agency's intransigence. By shutting Evergreen down when we have an acquisition deal approved by the MIA that would also result in Evergreen being the first CO-OP to repay any of the $2.4 billion CMS had mismanaged, CMS would be eliminating one of only two major competitors to CareFirst on the Maryland Exchange. CareFirst will have virtually unlimited ability to raise their premiums to whatever level they want, making CMS's comments to the press about encouraging more competition ring terribly false.
>
> Evergreen urges CMS to favorably consider Evergreen's proposal of the previous night—to buy out the CMS loan at $0.05 on the $1.00 and to let Evergreen go on as a non-profit HMO in Maryland, eventually undergoing a conversion and acquisition subject only to oversight of the Maryland Insurance Administration.

Amazingly, within thirty minutes of sending the email, Counihan called to say that CMS and the various federal agencies that had to sign off on the idea were considering it and he would get back to me in an hour.

When Counihan did not respond in a timely fashion, I sent a comparably worded memo to President Obama's chief of staff, Denis McDonough, making a similar plea to avert bad news for Obamacare by supporting our proposal and asking him to weigh in with Slavitt to urge him and the various relevant federal agencies to approve our proposal.

Within an hour, Matt Lynch called Redmer and me to let us know that CMS was now very seriously considering our deal. In fact, they were likely (though don't interpret this as guaranteed, he said) to send us the terms of a deal that they would accept by the end of the week. The terms:

- CMS would accept five cents on the dollar ($3.275 million) to buy out the CMS loan, and we would be released from CMS control.
- Until the $8 million loan was funded we couldn't sell on the Obamacare exchange (we would be "suppressed").
- Going forward, we'd be free to complete our acquisition transaction and conversion to for-profit by simply working in concert with Commissioner Redmer and Maryland law.
- Receivership would be on hold until a decision on this deal was made.

Expected closure would be no later than November 30, 2016, and Evergreen would be suppressed from the marketplace until the deal had been closed. With the exception of being kept off the exchange, this was exactly what we had been proposing for months.

Suppression meant the temporary forced removal of Evergreen from Maryland's individual exchange, which would begin open enrollment on November 1. We would be hurt if we were suppressed for a long period, because much of our growth in 2017 would come from the individual exchange, where we now had the lowest-priced policies in the market. We were able to accomplish this for two reasons: (1) CareFirst had raised their individual policy rates by about 45% over the past two years (to offset the huge loss they had suffered with this sector of the market when they had so severely underpriced the market at the outset of the ACA); and (2) our premiums remained relatively flat, as we offered some of the most comprehensive policies that rewarded preventive behaviors of subscribers with chronic conditions, saving the CO-OP money (due to the expected decrease in unnecessary hospitalizations and emergency visits). However, if the agreement could be reached expeditiously we might be able to get back on the individual exchange within a few days of its opening. This was because our investors were ready to fund the $8 million loan, and we could fund the $3 million buyout of the CMS note within a day of signing an agreement with CMS.

Ren Tundermann spent the following day, October 26, swiveling between the two investor groups (JARS and AAHS), Commissioner Redmer, and me, taking all sides into account as she wrote up the legal agreement to get Evergreen out from under the control of CMS. The "definitive agreement" was finished at 9:30 p.m., and I quickly forwarded it to Matt Lynch.

Waiting, as usual, for news from CMS, we didn't hear anything until 5 p.m. the next day, when Lynch called me. CMS saw no problems with the agreement I had sent them, but a final decision couldn't be reached until early next week because four other federal agencies—including DOJ and OMB—had to sign off. He promised to give me a call Monday afternoon to give me a solid sense of which way the decision was going to go. This was about the best we could have hoped for—again, if the feds agreed to our terms, we were ready to have the bridge loan funded and the CMS note bought, and we could be back on the exchange immediately thereafter.

I settled in for the evening, knowing there wasn't much to do until Monday.

On October 28, the four individual investors of JARS and the board of Anne Arundel Health System approved an additional $1 million each for the bridge loan, should we need it to take us to Redmer's new red line of 100% risk-based capital. With $10 million now pledged, plus our $3.275 million at the ready to buy out the CMS loan, Redmer tried to pressure CMS to deliver their verdict, so if we were approved, we could be on the exchange within a day or two of the start of open enrollment.

Then, a potentially damaging blow. Unbeknownst to us or Redmer, the Maryland Health Benefit Exchange (the state's Obamacare exchange) sent out the following email to the entire broker community of Maryland:

> Effective November 1, if a consumer tries to renew or enroll in an Evergreen plan for 2017, the following pop-up message will appear:
>
> Evergreen plans are not available at this time. Maryland Health Connection expects to know soon if Evergreen plans will become available before open enrollment for 2017 ends. It is important to choose a plan by Dec. 15 to ensure Jan. 1 coverage. If you choose a plan now with a different carrier, you may still switch to Evergreen if those plans become available prior to the end of open enrollment on Jan. 31.

They might as well have said "Evergreen won't survive, so don't sell their policies." Upon receiving a copy of this email from a concerned broker, I immediately called the executive director of the exchange, Jon Kromm. He was shocked that the email had gone out—not expecting to have to give any notice to brokers for several days. Although brokers predominately sold policies to groups, this missive would only serve to raise more doubts about our viability. Apology aside, we needed them to put out an immediate retraction, which they did.

I then spent several minutes with the investors, reassuring them that nothing had changed. I called Matt Lynch to tell him the email only heightened the need to get a final decision by Monday so that we could be on the exchange, which would greatly improve perceptions of our likelihood of survival. Al Redmer did the same, and reported to me that Lynch seemed to understand the urgency. Ren Tundermann then relayed that Lynch had told Redmer that our deal was expeditiously wending its way through the five federal agencies whose approval was required, and that if Lynch got the thumbs up by Monday, October 31, CMS would lift our suppression from the individual exchange.

But, one step forward and one step back, as we now had to deal with a self-inflicted wound. After several reviews of our financials, the MIA accounting staff found that we had booked $4 million more in premiums for the year than we had actually collected.

Apparently, our accounting staff had been counting premium revenue on an ongoing basis from clients who had actually dropped off our rolls due to lack of payment. In other words, they and our new third-party administrator had not been reconciling these actions. So now we were faced with this $4 million hit to our bottom line, which translated into about $4 million more (for a total of $12 million) that our investors had to come up with before the first of the year, to keep us at that required reserve level of 100% RBC (notice how the MIA continued to allow us to have progressively lower reserves and still avoid receivership).

Halloween was spent apologizing for our mistake to all the investors and trying to persuade them to stay on board. They all wanted to buy the company on the cheap, not realizing that, even with this additional $4 million, they were getting a good deal by buying this likely-to-be-profitable insurance company with almost 40,000 clients. Nevertheless, I had to bite the bullet and fall on my sword. It appeared that the effort was successful, as all investors seemed still to be on board at the end of the day.

CMS didn't meet their deadline of telling us by October 31 of the various federal agencies' decisions. In a call, Lynch told me that the ball had not moved a bit—the proposal was still with DOJ, and there was now absolutely no timetable for when a decision by that or any other agency would be made.

But one decision had been made because of their intransigence: we were off the exchange until further notice.

By Tuesday, the first day of November, JARS and AAHS had come to terms with the increase in funding needed due to the $4 million mistake, and remained solid on going forward with the deal. Now, we just needed CMS to allow us to go forward and get on the exchange.

As we knew would happen, an astute reporter from the *Baltimore Sun*, who picked up on the fact that Evergreen wasn't available for enrollment on the first day of the Maryland exchange, started asking questions. The MIA and Evergreen gave vague comments that seemed to satisfy her for the time being, but would not suffice for long. An extended period of suppression from the exchange would lead to major negative perceptions in the broker community, and if suppression lasted a long time, we were afraid that the investors would pull out.

I checked in with Lynch and Kevin Counihan at the end of the day, to see where things stood, and got an odd email communication from Lynch, in which he informed me that there was no update on when we'd get approval for our deal, *but* he still attached the copy of a complete letter on CMS letterhead that would be sent to us releasing us from CMS control—as soon as the decision had been made.

The next afternoon, I called Counihan to check on the status of our proposal. He assured me that although it was still stalled in DOJ, it was looking favorable, and he expected a decision shortly. But by the end of the week, there was still no movement. Interestingly, though, we got a detailed form from DOJ to fill out and return as soon as possible. It was clearly part of the process of paying off the loan. This, combined with the draft letter from CMS terminating our loan agreement, led me to believe that a positive decision on our proposal to buy out CMS was likely. The issue was whether the investors would maintain their interest in the transaction until next Friday. To that end, I was on the evening call between both sets of investors to update them on the CMS/DOJ process. After I got off the call, they were to discuss whether they had the stomach for staying in the game for another week.

Later on the evening of November 3, Tori Bayless, the CEO of Anne Arundel Health System, called to inform me that they were not comfortable with the risk that a decision wouldn't be made soon. They were very sorry, but they were no longer willing to invest or loan any money. Thinking we were headed for receivership yet again, I came into work the next day with an attitude of resignation.

However, a quick call from Mark Puente said that JARS was all in, and another call to Redmer sent the roller coaster back up again. Redmer was gung-ho that we should keep trying to solve the problem, even with AAHS apparently out of the picture. What would we do to replace AAHS's $4 million? Apparently, he wasn't too concerned about that.

I reached Lynch on election eve, November 7, to ask him for an update. He said there was no word on the likelihood of a positive response or on the timeline for such a decision, although it might be by the end of the following week.

Good news to start Election Day—our actuaries from Milliman came back with a very positive updated estimate of our likely risk adjustment payment for the coming year. Their most likely estimate was $6.5 million—a full $6 million less than previously estimated. Just like that, it appeared that we no longer needed the full $8-plus million in bridge loans to get us to the 100% RBC surplus level that the MIA required before the deal closed. I immediately sent this report to Redmer and our investment partners, to which Redmer replied that his staff would get to work immediately to verify Milliman's findings.

Bad news to end Election Day—by early Wednesday morning, November 9, 2016, it became clear that Donald Trump had won the 2016 presidential election—harnessing the anger and frustration of white working- and middle-class voters in the middle of the country, the South, and even part of the upper Midwest. Arguments will be made about what Hillary Clinton could have done differently, but I am convinced that the flames of disdain and mistrust of Obamacare fanned by the Republicans among these Trump voters, which coincided with their general feeling that the government does not work for them, but rather for "others," fed into that anger and helped to doom Clinton's bid to be president.

Had the implementation of the Affordable Care Act gone more smoothly this would perhaps not have been the case, but we will never know, because Obamacare's implementation was terribly flawed. It is true that rabid Republican congressional opposition to the ACA kept the Obama administration from proposing legislative changes (for fear of Republican mischief-making with a reopened bill). However, the fault for many of the deficiencies of the

ACA rollout, from the disastrous start of the federal and several state exchanges, to the exit of major carriers from many exchanges, to the failure of most of the CO-OPs (which constituted the majority of new competitors spawned by the ACA), fell squarely at the feet of CMS and its parent agency, HHS.

As this terribly distressing election result sunk in, I postulated what the Trump win might mean for Evergreen. Clearly, with Trump's campaign promise to immediately repeal and replace Obamacare, the ACA's survival was in serious doubt. However, it wouldn't be easy to dismantle the entire ACA, since the many parts of the law were now deeply entangled in the overall fabric of the American health system. Indeed, that was what eventually transpired when the Republican-controlled Congress was not able to repeal or replace the ACA in dozens of votes throughout 2017. Instead, discrete portions of the ACA would eventually be surgically excised (for example, the tax penalty required to be assessed on Americans without insurance—the so-called individual mandate—was zeroed out as part of the GOP tax bill at the end of 2017). The elimination of the CO-OP program would certainly be considered by the new administration. Long term, Evergreen would have to develop plans that would enable us to address the financial concerns of those who lost their insurance as a consequence of changes to the ACA enacted by the Republicans. But first, we would have to survive to get to that point.

Unsure of what would ensue with Trump's election, Al Redmer and I made a strong push to Matt Lynch to get CMS to do everything they could to get our loan buyout proposal approved by DOJ, so that we could be out from under CMS before Trump's transition team started looking into CMS and the CO-OP program. Thinking that CMS might like to have at least one CO-OP continue, we hoped for the best.

While we continued to wait on CMS and DOJ for some inkling of a decision, individuals were still not allowed to enroll in Evergreen on the Maryland exchange. Meanwhile, George Nemphos (the JARS group's attorney) let us know that his investor group wanted assurances that we wouldn't lose too much individual enrollment during our time off the exchange. We gave him information on the small number who had enrolled with other carriers to date along with financial projections based on various percentages of our expected individual enrollment that might be lost due to continued suppression.

While in the meeting, our attorneys for the federal lawsuit, Caroline Brown and Phil Peisch, informed us that they had been approached by the DOJ attorneys who had been involved in our federal court case, wanting them to find out if we would be willing to dismiss our risk adjustment case in return for DOJ approving our buyout deal. Brown and Peisch referred the feds to me. Meanwhile, Lynch also called to tell me of this promising new development. Wanting to move expeditiously, I asked him when DOJ would be calling. He said he would send me a new draft of our agreement to terminate the CMS loan, which would include the dismissal of the case. As soon as I got it, I sent an immediate reply, saying that we accepted the new language.

According to Lynch, DOJ would process this information and make a "quick" decision—which now would need the principal deputy attorney general's sign-off. Unfortunately, the next day, Friday, was Veterans Day, but Lynch assured me that DOJ would be working on this regardless. His prediction: we would have approval Monday and could be put back on the exchange Tuesday. I took this timeline with a grain of salt, but it seemed promising, although I continued to observe my philosophy of "never get too high or too low."

Why the sudden "hurry up"? I didn't know for sure, but the fact that the Trump transition team would be coming into CMS early the next week likely gave the current administration significant impetus to get this deal out the door before the new administration put the kibosh on it.

With CMS missing a deadline again, I tried Lynch on Tuesday for an update. No response to more than a dozen calls to Lynch, Counihan, and Slavitt. It was not until Al Redmer called me at 5 p.m. to tell me that Lynch had just called him (expressing his apology for not calling me directly) to let him know that there was now a "cone of silence" over DOJ, and CMS was no longer allowed to communicate with us while the DOJ process was in progress.

I went to Washington on Wednesday, November 16, for what would likely be the last meeting of NASHCO, the national association of CO-OPs. We met with Republican healthcare lobbyists to hear their prognostications regarding potential CMS/HHS appointees, as well as the upcoming administration's health policy. At the end of the meeting, the remaining CO-OP CEOs met with Lynch. I hadn't talked to him for a few days, but I took this opportunity to try to get a little intelligence on DOJ's verdict. All I found out was that indeed it seemed that CMS no longer had any influence over the decision on our deal.

The next serious threat to Evergreen appeared on the near horizon. Redmer asked Jon Kromm, the executive director of the Maryland Health Benefit

Exchange, how much longer Evergreen's automatic enrollment could be on hold before existing individual Evergreen enrollees were required to switch insurers in order to be eligible for coverage on January 1. Kromm responded that the end of November was the absolute deadline. The reason: if we weren't approved to go on the individual exchange, our current 8,000 enrollees in the individual market would have to be given time to change their insurer before coverage would start on January 1, 2017.

Using this information, Redmer followed up with an email to Lynch expressing, yet again, the urgency for a quick decision from DOJ. The pressure may have worked. Regardless, on Wednesday, November 23, Lynch called to inform me that the DOJ had approved our deal to get out from under the federal government's control. He told me to expect some official papers from DOJ in the next couple of days to complete the agreement, and he asked me to keep quiet about the news until he had told Redmer of CMS's decision to allow us back on the exchange.

So, as Thanksgiving approached, we were on the verge of success—the Hail Mary pass launched a few weeks earlier had been caught at the one-yard line, and our wide receiver was lunging for the goal line. A touchdown awaited.

We now set out to determine how we'd move forward when the promised approval of the deal occurred. On December 1, our Evergreen team and the JARS contingent boarded the elevator to attend a meeting with the MIA top staff and Commissioner Redmer, intending to come to a conclusion on the actual financial requirements of JARS to move forward. In the ensuing two hours, we squabbled over financials, the veracity of our risk adjustment estimates, and possible scenarios should JARS pull out after doing due diligence. We came to consensus on the financial and risk adjustment issues—agreeing on a total need from JARS of $13 million before closing in March, with some flexibility on timing of the payments.

Much of the time was spent on contingency plans should JARS walk away from the deal if they found any heretofore unknown major problems with the company's situation. They had a $7 million incentive to stay in the deal (the JARS investors' collective contribution to the bridge loan, which they would be unlikely to recoup if they walked away). However, Redmer had us play out what would happen if the deal didn't come to fruition, and yet we had enrolled individuals on the exchange in December and were put in receivership in January. We replied that if this happened, the estimated 8,000 such individuals would have to be allowed time to switch insurance companies so they would be insured starting February 1. This meant that we would be on the hook to cover the cost of their care for the month of January. We assured the commissioner we had more than enough cash on hand to do so.

Taking this information into consideration, we reached a tentative deal: Redmer would allow us on the exchange now, as long as the investors put in the first $7 million immediately. Due diligence would have to be completed by JARS by December 19 and a go/no-go decision made by the investors at that time. If a go, then the MIA would require additional injections of capital to titrate us to a 75% RBC reserve level (an even lower level of reserves than previously required by the MIA to keep us out of disciplinary action) until we got to closing, when JARS would inject the capital to get us to the going concern surplus level of 200% RBC. If a no-go, the MIA would work with the Maryland exchange to transfer the several thousand individual Evergreen enrollees to other carriers in time for new coverage on January 1.

All good, until, late in the meeting, one of Redmer's staff suddenly brought up an astounding contention that CMS had made to them in a call the day before. CMS had notified the MIA that by not paying our risk adjustment payment in full, when assessed, we would be turned over to the federal Treasury Department for being in arrears and charged a 30% penalty on the outstanding balance: at least $7 million! That made absolutely no sense, as CMS, in the person of Matt Lynch, had explicitly offered us the option—which we took—to pay back the risk adjustment assessment monthly by netting out federal subsidies owed Evergreen each month against the balance of the risk adjustment payment, without ever mentioning any such condition. This was clearly a deal-breaker, if it proved to be true. Nemphos, Tundermann, and I stared at each other in disbelief upon hearing this news.

Surprisingly, the meeting adjourned without further addressing this potentially catastrophic development—it just sat there like an elephant in the room. We left, and disconsolately headed back to Evergreen to see what we could find out about this 30% penalty.

After some searching, we found a dunning letter that had gone to Manny Sheldon. Upon reading the fine print, we saw that it mentioned the requirement for CMS to refer a debt not paid in full for more than ninety days. The debt would be referred to the United States Department of Treasury for collection, with a penalty of up to 30% on the balance owed. Lynch had disclosed nothing about this to Manny when the offsetting was approved—a rather significant omission. Now we were worried that we were dead in the water. This sentiment intensified after I talked to Reed Cleary at CMS, who confirmed that they had talked to the MIA and told them that we would be turned over to Treasury to recoup the 30% interest.

Back at Evergreen headquarters, our general counsel, Mary Porter, and I raced to find the part of federal law—31 US Code Sect 3711(g), to be exact— that was cited in the dunning letter, related to collection of debts owed the government.

It was fortunate that we did this, as it would immediately become clear to any literate person who read the relevant portion of the law that CMS's assertion that our debt had to be referred to the Treasury was completely wrong. In looking at the list of qualified exemptions to referral of a debt, it was obvious that we qualified for not one, but two exemptions from paying interest: we were still in litigation over risk adjustment; and we were offsetting in sufficient amounts to pay the full claim to the government in well under one year.

As relieved as I was to discover that we were free and clear, I was struck by the realization that, if we hadn't researched the relevant part of federal law, Evergreen would have been assessed a deal-breaking penalty and would have had to close up shop due to an erroneous assertion by an uninformed bureaucrat.

I called Lynch to let him know of our analysis of the law. I also asked him why he hadn't mentioned the huge penalty that would hit us. He said he hadn't been aware of it until a few days earlier, when another division of CMS notified him that we owed the 30% penalty as part of the finalization of our buyout deal.

In other words, our parent agency had encouraged us to pay off our $24 million risk adjustment assessment on a monthly basis (by foregoing about $3 million a month owed to us for federal premium subsidies for lower-income enrollees) without telling us that such an agreement would result in a penalty of over $7 million—because they didn't know about it. And then, at the last moment, they sprang this on us and our investors just as the decision about the deal was being finalized. Even worse, Evergreen would have been shut down had we not researched the law ourselves and found that CMS was dead wrong.

On December 6, Redmer came to Evergreen for a quick visit, which I used as an opportunity to have the entire staff thank him for all his efforts on our behalf during the past year; and to unveil the plaque naming our conference room for the commissioner.

Since nothing was ever easy or completely positive throughout this seemingly never-ending roller-coaster ride, after we feted Redmer, he and I adjourned to my office, where he presented me with a commissioner's order requiring any expenditure greater than $10,000 going forward to be preapproved by MIA, and for good measure, also ordering us to cease selling individual plans off the exchange, as well as keeping us suppressed from the exchange for the time being (until JARS ponied up the required cash).

By the end of the day, however, after a few more edits, Tundermann reported that the MIA had approved of the terms of the deal, and the entire JARS group was to discuss it in their nightly call.

The next day Tundermann called to tell me that JARS had made yet another change in its terms. Now they required Evergreen to pay for all diligence up until December 30, and they would not put the first $3.5 million in until that date passed without a major adverse finding. Thus, we would have to delay paying off our CMS loan until the last day of the year (fortunately, CMS had continued its well-worn pattern of significantly missing their deadlines, as we hadn't yet received either of the formal documents they had initially pledged to send some time ago; thus, we couldn't pay off our loan to them yet, anyway). In addition, JARS wanted to continue to put off injecting any more capital until the MIA completed its preliminary risk adjustment estimates in March.

Not adding to the surplus until March meant we would not be on the individual market—on or off the exchange—at all in 2017. This would create the domino effect of dramatically decreasing our panel of patients seen at the PCOs, since over half of their patients came from Evergreen's individual market members. This was particularly concerning since so many of those patients had chosen the PCOs for their robust care and were receiving excellent primary and behavioral care (often for the first time in years). They would now likely lose that care when they were forced to choose another insurer, since only Evergreen enrollees could use the PCOs.

In addition to the deleterious effect on the PCOs, the new JARS plan also caused concern among the CO-OP's employees. Having spent much of the past year in a state of constant stress and fear of the CO-OP going under, this new timetable (which would result in closing the transaction in May at the earliest) meant Evergreen staff would be in limbo for at least another half a year. Although the morale of the staff was remarkably good considering the circumstances, another six months of constant angst might well take a toll.

By December, the investors had lost confidence in Manny Sheldon, due to the fact that our actual financials did not always fall in line—occasionally significantly. In his defense, this monthly differential of actuals to projections is often part of the nature of the industry, where claims may vary by 20% from month to month, particularly with a company like ours, with a relatively small total enrollment. Nevertheless, Manny was released in mid-month.

The investors looked prescient when the November actuals showed a modest loss rather than the $500,000 profit Manny had assured us we would see. Once again, I had to go back to the investors to ask for their forbearance. I spent much of the ensuing week in discussions with JARS's attorney, George Nemphos, and a couple of the investors. We continued to provide them with scenario after scenario to help them get comfortable with our financial projections, but they remained skittish.

Meanwhile, Redmer was balking at JARS's request to have Evergreen pay for their due diligence efforts. He was opposed to this because Evergreen would lose precious resources that would be needed to pay its enrollees' medical claims should the deal not go through and a wind-down was begun.

Still, on December 8, the commissioner held a morning press briefing to announce that Evergreen was going to go forward and that a deal was in process. A torrent of press calls followed. After doing a slew of interviews, the articles were all posted online by noon, and we were quite pleased with the coverage. Frankly, the coverage was far more positive than we had any right to expect. The *Sun*'s article was particularly favorable, stating that Evergreen expected to finalize an agreement with CMS that would require it to pay off a portion of its $65 million startup loan in exchange for separating from CMS's oversight, and that I hoped to finalize the conversion in April or May, at which time Evergreen would be in a much stronger financial position than ever before.

This led me to send the following to Nemphos: "Below are the links to media coverage of today's MIA announcement . . . all in all, much better than we had expected. Broker reaction has been supportive to very positive, per Dustin, our sales chief. This includes the Kelly brothers, who run the biggest

TPA in the state—Dustin met with them after the release came out and they were very supportive. Hope this is reassuring to JARS!"

By now, we were becoming insistent that JARS get their auditors in to finish diligence as soon as possible, as it was clear that if they did not inject their first tranche of the investment by January 1, the commissioner would shut off any future group enrollment along with ceasing individual sales, effectively putting us out of business. Thus, all diligence had to be completed by the end of December to enable JARS to make the decision about whether to go forward (and put in $3.5 million) or bail (and send us into receivership). Indeed, Redmer was getting increasingly frustrated with the lack of urgency displayed by JARS, but closed an email to me with a jaunty, "Keep hope alive!!!," highlighting his innate optimism.

Things took a turn for the worse in mid-December, on a conference call with Mark Puente and Chris Brandt. As several of our senior staff sat around the table in our large conference room, we stared at each other in disbelief as Brandt told us that he thought the deal had gotten too risky, and there was no way he could see to raise the $13 to $17 million needed to complete the acquisition. No reason was given, despite repeated assurances from JARS and Nemphos, their attorney, as recently as earlier that week, that they were good for the totality of the investment needed. In constant communication with Nemphos, Tundermann was absolutely flabbergasted. Confronting him with this information, she was informed that he thought JARS was still in it.

Now on our fifth cat (having exhausted somewhere north of thirty-six lives), this was yet another existential crisis. Immediately jumping on the phone, we went back to some of our previous suitors to see if they might be interested in being part of the acquisition. Trusted Health in DC: no; Tori Bayless of Anne Arundel Health System: no. A quick check again with Oscar Health out of New York City also bore no fruit—they were impressed by our operation and our model, and indeed, Oscar wanted to come to the Washington-Baltimore market in the next couple of years, but the timing just wasn't right.

The day ended with me chairing a late afternoon board meeting of our PCOs (which had their own nonprofit organization). Informing the PCO board of the dire straits in which the CO-OP found itself, I encouraged them to start contingency planning to save the PCOs. Since each of the PCO's panels of patients was primarily made up of Evergreen CO-OP members, without a solution, the PCOs would cease to exist as well. Two options emerged: (1) get a contract to provide primary care to members of other insurance carrier(s) and/or Medicare; or (2) sell the PCOs and their providers to an interested party, such as a medical system.

I checked in with Puente and Nemphos to see where they were. They were skittish, but still tenuously hanging in there. I quizzed them on what they needed before they decided, by the end of the following week, whether they would or would not inject the first round of funding. We ended the call agreeing that we would continue along this path of completing financial diligence and pursuing potential additional investors for the next week and a half and see where we stood at the deadline of the end of the month.

During the last ten days of December, it became obvious that we were going to have to find more investors ourselves to come up with the requisite monies to take the deal forward. Except for Puente, few of the JARS team were doing anything proactively to seek out other investors.

As we pursued targets, I queried Puente and Nemphos as to what it would take in terms of new investment to bring Brandt back in and get JARS to commit to going forward. The answer: "firm pledge(s) totaling at least $3 million." With our goal now defined, we began calling potential investors.

We quickly narrowed down the pool to an A list of those individuals/entities that understood the health insurance world, knew the Maryland market, and could quickly invest at least $500,000, knowing that Al Redmer's immense patience could not be tested too much longer. To that end, we set a goal of obtaining commitments of $3 million by the end of the first week of January (Redmer's new deadline).

Although a handful of the dozen A listers removed themselves from consideration quickly, a good half dozen looked very promising. With these, and a few other potential financiers in the mix, by December 28 I felt confident enough to go back to Matt Lynch to ascertain CMS's current posture on the process of loan forgiveness and our exit from the CO-OP program. He let me know that as soon as a final term sheet for the deal was presented to CMS, such letters forgiving the loan and removing us from CMS supervision would be sent. Our payoff of the CMS loan would have to follow within twenty-four hours.

I informed the team from Evergreen and JARS, and urged us all to get a term sheet finalized by the end of the first week of January. Time was running out with the feds, since the Trump administration would take office in three weeks, and a completely different CMS could be expected—one that would likely not follow through with the Obama administration's deal with us. Extra emphasis was placed on securing additional commitments so that JARS would be comfortable to go forward with the deal and free up the $3.275 million needed to pay off the CMS loan.

Chapter Twelve

Ten Frenzied Days

January 2017

Everything seemed to be coming down to the wire. On January 4, an email from Matt Lynch informed me of some new time-sensitive requirements before our proposed deal could be accepted. We needed yet another version of the term sheets to get to the feds as soon as possible, and we had to send a formal request for a waiver of an interest payment on our outstanding risk adjustment balance newly identified by CMS. The request had to explain why collecting interest on the balance was "against equity and good conscience," or why assessing interest is "against the best interest of the U.S."

Oh, and by the way, Lynch informed me that to date, no such waivers had been granted to anyone under this process. I asked Ren Tundermann to prepare the timeline for the remaining risk adjustment payments and the letter requesting a waiver of the interest on that remaining risk adjustment obligation. As usual, she came through, and we sent those two items along with our now-completed final term sheets to CMS by the end of the day.

On a lark, I reached out the night of January 6 to the CEO of Anne Arundel Health System, Tori Bayless, to take her temperature about rejoining the investor group. To address her previous concerns, I filled her in on our successes in the more financially favorable group market, and our very successful efforts at risk score optimization to reduce our risk adjustment liability. She replied immediately that she "was intrigued," and she asked for financials and term sheets to take to her senior staff.

Getting the materials to her within the hour, I quickly heard back that she wanted to discuss things further. Although JARS had been requiring any additional investor to fund the escrow account by early the following week, I told Bayless (and confirmed with JARS) that a firm written commitment of $2 to $3 million by early next week would suffice to get JARS to inject the initial tranche of funding and move forward with the deal.

With Bayless's interest piqued, things were looking up slightly. That balloon was punctured late in the afternoon, when I received an email from Al Redmer, letting me know that Lynch had called him to say that he could not proceed with sending our deal to other federal agencies for their approval until he had the Maryland Insurance Administration's blessing. Despite his longstanding efforts on our behalf, Redmer couldn't do that at the time, because we hadn't sent the MIA our November financials, which were the basis of our 2017 projections, on which MIA had to opine—and without the MIA's approval, our debt would be referred to the Treasury in five days.

The lack of November financials was our fault (though we were just one day late with them), and the MIA could quickly approve our term sheets and turn them back to CMS. The big issue here was Lynch's contention that we only had five days before our remaining risk adjustment obligation was turned over—yet again—to the US Treasury for collection of 30% interest on the balance owed (several million dollars). The reason this time: we had been in arrears for more than the 180 days allowed by statute. We had been here before—just a couple of months earlier—when CMS admitted it was wrong in its assertion that it should turn us over to the Treasury.

So, again, I went to the law books, where the language—again—supporting our not having to make the interest payment was plainly evident. A summary of my findings was included in an email to Lynch:

> It appears that you think that CMS is going to refer our RA payment obligation to Treasury in five days. This cannot be true for two reasons:
>
> a) 31 US Code Sect. 3711(g)(1) states that a period of 180 days is required for referral of a debt to Treasury. Our RA invoice was received August 12, 2016—180 days from that date is February 8, 2017, not five days from now;

in addition:

b) 31 US Code Sect. 3711(g)(2)(a)(i) states that no debt can be forwarded to Treasury for "any debt or claim that is in litigation." Our lawsuit is still in force with the Federal District Court of Maryland until the deal with CMS is signed, thus precluding any referral to Treasury.

What was particularly maddening about this episode was not so much the specifics of the mistake on the time period (anyone knows six months from the August invoice is February, not January), or missing the caveat about the continued litigation (for a second time!), or even requiring us to jump through hoops by needing the approval of more federal agencies (though that made no sense). What was so infuriating about these additional obstacles to our success was the time period in which it was occurring—only fifteen days before Donald Trump's inauguration. Along with the already seated Republican majorities in the House and Senate, the incoming president had vowed to dismantle the Obama administration's signature accomplishment—the ACA— as a first order of business.

Yet, with President Obama's prized achievement in tremendous danger, what was the agency tasked with the implementation of the entirety of the ACA doing in the last two weeks of the president's term? Were they promulgating regulations to make it harder to dismantle the ACA? No. Were they talking with congressional Democrats to provide them with arguments to use in public debates about the value of the ACA? No. They were spending their precious last few days in office creating more obstacles to the potential survival of one of the few remaining CO-OPs that had been placed in their charge.

While waiting to hear the results of the board meeting at Anne Arundel Health Systems regarding a possible investment, on Monday, January 9, I reached out to Neil Meltzer, the CEO of LifeBridge Health, a regional health system in central Maryland. Although turned down by their CFO the previous week, I knew that Meltzer had just arrived home from a vacation. Having had a good relationship with him since my days as Baltimore City health commissioner, I thought I should pitch a $2 to $3 million investment opportunity to him. I also happened to mention that AAHS was seriously looking at participating in the deal. This potential for a collaborative effort against the three giant health systems operating in the state—Johns Hopkins, University of Maryland, and

MedStar—clearly caught his attention. His CFO, David Krajewski, now encouraged by his boss, started throwing questions at us, fast and furious, to get up to speed.

By mid-afternoon, Anne Arundel's board meeting was over. I didn't immediately hear from Tori Bayless, but AAHS's counsel called George Nemphos and Ren Tundermann to set up a meeting to discuss the terms of the deal—which we took as a good sign. A call from Bayless early in the evening partially confirmed that hunch—but only partially. It seemed that AAHS was indeed strongly considering an investment—potentially as the "deep pocket" investor, which would eventually cover a majority of the required capital over the next two years. However, in their initial discussions with JARS's lawyers, two issues were stumbling blocks. JARS wanted sole control of the details of the acquisition deal; and AAHS wanted a more equal role in governance of the new entity, in terms of board seats, especially considering their hope to eventually become the majority owner of Evergreen.

I told Bayless that I was sure that Nemphos and Tundermann would compromise somewhat on working on the deal, and there was room for discussion on governance. However, as Bayless recognized, one had to keep in mind that JARS had stayed in for the long run, while AAHS had literally pulled the rug out from under JARS and Evergreen back in November. I also asked her how she felt about LifeBridge being interested in joining the investor consortium. Though LifeBridge was not the perfect partner, she allowed that it made some sense, but she would wait to see what transpired with them.

The next day started with an email from Lynch, informing me that, indeed, we were correct about the law, and our interest payment was *not* being referred to the Treasury, and, one hoped, never would be. But there was a fly in the ointment: although the Department of Justice had signed off on the term sheets for the deal previously, they asked to review them again. However, he assured me, that even with this step, CMS should still be ready to terminate our loan agreement with the federal government in the next few days.

I know, I know—why would I expect an expeditious review from any federal agency? Because it was our only hope.

On January 11, we heard from both AAHS and LifeBridge Health. In a sudden embarrassment of riches, LifeBridge expressed a strong desire to join the investor consortium and invest in the deal at an equal level with AAHS, which in turn agreed to match what JARS was putting up. At the same time, the three investors in JARS who had removed their money from escrow a few weeks earlier reconsidered and were restoring their shares to the JARS escrow account. In one day, we had gone from a pledged $3.5 million from three of the original JARS participants, to at least $5.5 million from JARS, $5.5 million from AAHS, and $1 million immediately from LifeBridge (which would increase its contribution to match AAHS and JARS's current and future investments after they did due diligence of their own).

With over $10 million in hand, we would be able to fund both the buyout of the CMS loan and bolster our drained reserve account. We would also have a few million dollars left over to fulfill the injection of additional capital required by the MIA in order to bring our risk-based capital up to 75%. Now, if only CMS would let us know when we would be able to close out their part of the bargain. CMS had been under constant harassment from Redmer and me over the past few days, with the likes of the following missive: "Matt—I've left a couple of messages; we're ready to go. We need to receive the two letters from you guys and instructions on how to wire the $3.275 M to buy out the CMS loan. Please get them to us ASAP. Thanks, pb." Apparently, it worked, for right in the middle of talking with our potential investors around noon, I got an email from Lynch at CMS that laid out an expeditious timeline for termination of our federal loan and our removal from federal oversight.

Exactly what we had asked for. Although previous experience urged caution, I gave a gleeful shout in the privacy of my office, before calling Redmer to let him know the potentially very good news. This, combined with AAHS, LifeBridge, and JARS coming together, meant we were tantalizingly close to a complete deal. It was time to update the entire investment team of where we stood:

1. On the CMS front—Matt Lynch had sent a timeline which allowed us to meet Al Redmer's Jan. 15 deadline for CMS approval and funding.
2. On the MIA front, Al Redmer was all in, and will send MIA approval to Matt Lynch, as long as we are ready to invest $6 million by Friday, 1/13.
3. On the investor front:
   a) as of this moment, AAHS is willing to put in $$ equal to JARS, creating at least the $9 million JARS requires to go forward with the first $6 million tranche.
   b) LifeBridge is "very intrigued" and is contemplating matching JARS and AAHS to create a tripartite structure.

4. Next steps:
   a) finalize investors' contributions
   b) Get signatures on term sheets / surplus note purchase agreements / intercompany creditor agreements, surplus notes
   c) investors wire funds to Evergreen
   d) Evergreen wires $3.275 million to CMS
   e) Evergreen pays commitment fee to each investor

The day ended with George Nemphos, Ren Tundermann, Mark Puente, Jonathan Burklund, Roberta Hurst, and me plotting out the activities that needed to happen to end our relationship with the federal government and to satisfy our insurance commissioner's financial requirements by the close of business on Friday, two days hence.

By noon the next day, I started pestering Lynch: "Hi Matt—just checking in on when we will get the termination letter scheduled for today?" After eight unanswered phone calls over the next six hours, I changed tone, so at 6:36 p.m., Lynch got the following from me: "We were told we would get the CMS termination letter today. We have not yet received it. We have all our investors' money ready to be deposited tomorrow, and our $3.275 million ready to be sent via ACH to CMS tomorrow. (If need be, I will deliver a check to you personally in Bethesda tomorrow.) Please stick to your timetable; it is critical to get this done tomorrow. Thank you." Two minutes later I received an apology from Lynch and an assurance that we would get a revised timeline for receiving the termination letter shortly.

We began the next day, Friday the 13th, waiting to hear if it would be good or bad luck for Evergreen. About 9:30 a.m., Lynch called to tell me he had good news and bad news. The good news was that CMS had approved the two letters (one terminating our status as a CO-OP and the other forgiving the balance on our CMS loan) necessary to get us out of our relationship with the federal government. The bad news was that the Trump transition team was at the Department of Justice today considering all deals that were in process.

Why DOJ had to reapprove the deal—the same terms they had approved four weeks earlier—made absolutely no sense. I asked why the Trump administration had any say about our deal prior to their taking power on Inauguration Day, a week away. Why would the Obama administration's DOJ care one whit what the incoming DOJ staff thought about our deal, since it would be completed by the inauguration? Lynch said he was just as frustrated as I was (I highly doubt it), and that he'd call Redmer to update him on the snag in the plan.

Lynch didn't call the insurance commissioner and didn't return my calls for several hours. Meanwhile, JARS, LifeBridge, and AAHS had signed off on the deal and were ready to immediately send us the first tranche of $6 million. I continued to worry that every day that went by without a conclusion allowed for the possibility of a deal-killing development.

All this was mind-boggling, particularly when one looked at what was about to confront the country. With the incoming president so disinterested in governing that he openly boasted about not needing to get daily intelligence briefings on threats to the American people and the world at large, why would his incoming administration care about a miniscule issue like a single CO-OP converting to a for-profit and returning taxpayer dollars?

Having signed all the documents and agreements between Evergreen and JARS/AAHS/LifeBridge and securing official approval of the MIA, I continued to wait for the last two pieces of the deal—the two letters from CMS. As the afternoon wore on, I got more and more frustrated at hearing nothing. Jokingly, I called Redmer and asked him if he'd call the governor and see if we could get a tank from the National Guard to storm CMS headquarters in Bethesda. With a laugh, Redmer promised he'd start shaking Lynch's cage.

Finally, I called Kevin Counihan, the #2 official at CMS. When I asked him why the Obama administration's CMS officials were even broaching the deal with the Trump CMS and DOJ transition teams when the Trump team had no authority to touch the deal at this time, he said that "leadership wanted to tell the Trump team." Counihan told me that the Obama CMS team and the Trump CMS transition team were meeting this afternoon, specifically about the Evergreen deal—though he wouldn't tell me who was at the meeting, nor when it was being held—and he denied my request to attend. Not divulging any information, he hung up, promising to call me that evening with the results of the meeting.

Worried that the deal was again in serious jeopardy, I reached out to Senator Cardin's chief of staff, Chris Lynch, who had been so helpful throughout our fifteen-month ordeal with CMS. I asked him to put some pressure on CMS to have the gumption to hold up their end of the bargain and do what most of the rest of the Obama administration's agencies were doing—finishing up any business before the Trump administration took office in one week.

At dinnertime, I finally got a call from Matt Lynch. Although the meeting was still going on between unnamed parties, "the smoke signals coming out of the meeting are positive." He wouldn't guarantee anything, but said it was likely that the two CMS letters (terminating us as a CO-OP and forgiving the remainder of the loan) would come to us Tuesday, allowing for the $3.275 million to buy out the loan to be sent to CMS Tuesday afternoon, January 17 (since Monday was Martin Luther King Jr. Day, a federal holiday). He was cagey in talking about any of the deliberations, but was clearly optimistic. He also confirmed with Redmer that the MIA would extend their deadline to fund to Tuesday. So, once again, we waited over a weekend to hear our fate.

I got a call from Matt Lynch on Sunday afternoon, January 15, while driving my youngest son, Hank. It was good news, as I related to our team: "Everything has been approved at the federal level. We are getting the two letters from CMS on Tuesday and our $3.275 m will be sent immediately thereafter (with the commissioner's approval of course). Still don't want to count chickens before they're hatched, but the beaks are showing through the shells."

Monday was spent nailing down all the inter-investor group agreements and making plans for wiring investor money to Evergreen and from Evergreen to CMS. Heading home, I finally let myself relax a bit, anticipating the completion of tomorrow's events, which would result in our escape from the clutches of CMS.

Relaxed too soon! A little before 8 p.m., I received a call from Counihan. In a surreal conversation, he informed me that there were issues with DOJ that had popped up at the end of last week. Issue briefs were circulating among the several federal agencies and the decision on our exit was stuck at CMS, DOJ, and OMB. We would not get our letters from CMS the next day, but he hoped to get back to me by close of business with an update. Rather confused by this direct contradiction to Matt Lynch's very clear message to me on Sunday, I asked Counihan how this could be—we had clearly been told that all agencies and the Trump transition team had given a green light to moving forward.

Counihan said: "I am not going to contradict what Matt said [really?], but this issue is not settled yet. We're going to get back to you as quickly as possible, can't tell you when, but it's at the top of the list for tomorrow."

Tomorrow no longer looked like such a good day.

Worried that the deal might get the kibosh at the last hour, I called Matt Lynch first thing Tuesday morning to see what had happened. In an "Alice in Wonderland" moment, without giving any explanation, he informed me that what he had told me still held true. The final presentation of our case had been made to the secretary of HHS that very morning at 8:30, and everything was a go.

Ironically, this agency, which had exasperated us with delay after delay, then laid out the following extremely rapid schedule for the day:

1:30: Letter sent to me terminating Evergreen as a CO-OP under the ACA's CO-OP program

2:00: Letter sent to me for signature, forgiving the balance of the CMS loan (all but the $3.275 million buyout)

2:30: The loan forgiveness letter comes back to CMS for countersignature

3:30: The $3.275 million wire to be sent to CMS (actual amount of five cents on the dollar: $3,272,545)

5:00: Press release to go out

Meanwhile, as soon as we got the first letter, all the investors had to send signed term sheets to Evergreen and the MIA. Upon receiving the signed term sheets signaling that the deal was going forward, the MIA would approve our request to be allowed to pay the $3.27 million.

The first letter came in at 1:25 p.m., prompting an email from me to Redmer: "Almost there—thanks for everything you have done to get us here! Remind me to tell you what happened with CMS last night when we have our meeting tomorrow." And back from him: "Anything to save your [Al Redmer] conference room."

The rest of the day was spent in a frenzy of activity—back and forth with CMS over the timing of our payment and intransigence on the part of AAHS's attorney. Needing the investors to sign off on the final documents from CMS, and then for MIA to allow us to sign the deal with CMS, we figured we had some time to do so, seeing as CMS got us the second letter at 2:30 that afternoon. As the process wound its way through the investor group, Lynch informed me at 4:45 that this was it.

"What do you mean?" I said.

"There is no more time; everything must be done today, no exception. You were actually turned down last Friday [!]; but then we got you approved [!!], and now everything must be done today [!!!]. You can't have any more time."

I called Ren Tundermann, who told JARS's attorney George Nemphos that all negotiations about board seats and governance among the investor groups had to stop, and all had to agree to the deal immediately. Amazingly, AAHS's attorney now raised concerns about a completely unimportant issue: the risk adjustment repayment plan.

At Nemphos's request, a few weeks earlier I had asked Matt Lynch if we could pay off the balance of our risk adjustment payment over a three-year period. Lynch acquiesced, and even got the prior interest on the balance waived. Now, the AAHS counsel was expressing reservations about this eminently reasonable process, which I had secured at the behest of the investors themselves.

Convinced that he was purposely killing the deal at the midnight hour, Nemphos and Tundermann took turns lambasting the AAHS attorney over his obstinacy. I called the AAHS COO Maulik Joshi (who had always supported the deal) and sent a string of increasingly urgent messages asking him to call me. He eventually did, and I literally pleaded with him to get his attorney to sign the deal—otherwise, years of hard work were going to go down the drain. Joshi promised to talk to him and get back to me quickly with the verdict.

At the same time as the AAHS lawyer was threatening to shut the deal down, Mark Puente called and offered to fund the entire first $6 million tranche himself. Unfortunately, the magnanimous offer by the investor who had done the most to keep the deal alive would come too late to satisfy CMS.

Finally, at 6:10 p.m., I got a terse text from AAHS's Maulik Joshi: "We are signing." Thank goodness. Now the documents all had to be signed by the investors and sent to the MIA for their approval. Then we could send the letter with my signature to CMS within the hour that we had left, per CMS's new deadline.

Racing against time, Nemphos and Tundermann gathered the documents and sent them to MIA. At 6:45 I got a text from Redmer: "Hey I spoke to Matt and talked him into the following . . . if the docs are signed tonight . . . and approved by Vinny and Van (MIA Staff) . . . and sent to him . . . and the press release is issued TONIGHT. Then we can do the wire transfer tomorrow am . . . Early."

I called Redmer, asking him what was so important to CMS about a press release having to go out so quickly. Indeed, Lynch was insistent that the release go out that day, no matter what time of night. Redmer replied that there was apparently a feeling at CMS/HHS that a press release documenting the completion of the deal would show it was not done on the eve of the inauguration.

After two more hours spent frantically chasing down signed agreements, they were all sent to the MIA, leading to the following communication from the agency: "Peter, the letter setting forth the MIA's approval of the surplus note is attached. The acquisition letter confirming the intention of the investor group to invest in Evergreen is acceptable, subject of course to the future submittal and review of the conversion application. Vinny."

My assistant, Jacob Petrini, immediately pressed the send button to transmit the final letter with my signature on its way to CMS. Countersigned by the CFO of CMS at 9:15 p.m., we were almost free of the agency that had "birthed" us, only to become our primary nemesis. And to satisfy CMS's oddly inexplicable requirement, we sent out our press release at 10:15 p.m.

Wednesday, January 18, was another crazy day. Amid press interviews on the deal, we frantically pursued the three investor groups to wire their money to us and give us proof of those wires. Doesn't sound too complicated, right? Wrong! Apparently, it was not so simple to track a wired payment unless you had a receipt with a federal reserve routing number on it—which delayed our ability to track any of the wires for several hours. All the while, I was fielding repeated texts from Matt Lynch asking, then pleading, and eventually demanding updates of our efforts. With a 4 p.m. deadline approaching for our wire to arrive at CMS, as they were insisting it must, the final wire receipt was found. We sent the three receipts to the MIA, proving the investors had funded Evergreen as required by the agency, and were immediately given approval to hit "send" on our request to our bank to wire funds in the amount of $3,272,545 to CMS. By 3:56 p.m. I had received three different calls from our bank asking me to confirm that we really did want to send the money.

By a mere four minutes, we met our deadline. With that, we were officially out from under the control of CMS. Now, we could start down the road to becoming a for-profit insurance company.

Chapter Thirteen

Finale

January to August 2017

Since the past tends to predict the future, it was no surprise that the path from Evergreen's release from CMS in early 2017 to Evergreen's intended eventual acquisition and conversion to a for-profit insurer was incredibly convoluted. First, for months LifeBridge and Anne Arundel Health Systems didn't allow us to disclose that they were two of our financial backers. Such information would have gone a long way toward establishing confidence in our viability among the broker community, which controlled much of our group enroll-ment. Instead, denied the identity of our investors, virtually every broker in the state remained very cautious about placing new business with us. In fact, we were not allowed to disclose the names of our investors for a full five months after getting out from under CMS. By that time, our enrollment had decreased month after month, from about 35,000 in November of 2016 to about 23,000 by June of 2017. This loss occurred largely because the Mary-land Insurance Administration prohibited us from selling individual policies on the Maryland ACA exchange from November 1 forward, so Evergreen's 10,000 or so individual market customers were not allowed to renew their policies with us. This dramatic decline led, obviously, to decreasing revenue and worsening finances.

Then, led by LifeBridge's CFO, David Krajewski, who had never understood the value of the PCOs, the investors decided not to take on the innovative and widely praised offices, eliminating one of the key differentiators Evergreen had going for it. This, too, raised red flags with brokers, who rightfully felt that putting business with a company that had just lost one of its major selling points was risky. Meanwhile, due diligence continued for months, with the investors continually delaying the closing of the deal, never being quite satisfied with the financial prospects of the company—which became a self-fulfilling prophecy the longer the delays went on.

The only aspect of the conversion process that went smoothly was the public hearing. Chaired by Al Redmer, the June 7 hearing provided all the ammunition he needed to approve the conversion. The reports of the independent consultants clearly showed that the preservation of Evergreen was in the public interest, the investors had the resources to move forward with the purchase, and there were no plans for the executives of Evergreen to gain equity or benefit from the transaction. The investors unanimously, and fervently, claimed that they were in it for the long haul. There was no opposition to the conversion, and Redmer ruled within days that the conversion to a for-profit and the broader acquisition were both approved by the MIA.

In a pleasant development, our contention to our potential investors that we would dramatically reduce our risk adjustment assessment proved true. On June 30, 2017, the 2016 risk adjustment assessments were released by CMS. Whereas our previous assessment was over $24 million, or 28.2% of our 2014 premium revenue, this year's assessment was just over $9 million, or 5.9% of our much larger 2015 premium revenue. Fulfilling our promise to radically reduce our risk adjustment payments, however, did little to push the investors along. Indeed, despite this immensely successful effort to chase codes and get our members to the doctor to improve our risk scores, which we assured them we could improve on for 2017, they largely expressed distrust of our abilities to do so.

Meanwhile, dragging out the process well into July had taken its toll: by creating overwhelming doubt about the future of Evergreen among the broker community, we were now suffering dramatically reduced group enrollment, which, in turn, created an increasingly fragile financial situation. In addition, as decreasing enrollment led to lower revenue, a claims backlog developed when we ran short of cash to promptly pay all claims. This, in turn, led to the need for additional capital to increase the reserve needed to cover all outstanding claims. All of these issues led to a steady increase in the funds required from the investor groups at closing to bring the company to a viable state. Needless to say, the investors bristled at this continued escalation of the overall cost of the deal.

And yet, the three groups continued to delay pulling the trigger and closing the deal, the absolute legal deadline (under the for-profit conversion law) for which was Thursday, July 28. This led to a chaotic period leading up to this cutoff date. The skittishness of the investors led Al Redmer to call an urgent meeting to put pressure on the parties to come to a conclusion. Despite the insurance commissioner's entreaties, the investors started raising the exact same questions about the financial sustainability of the company going forward that they had been asking since January. This was particularly irritating because we had gone through numerous audits of all our processes and finances over the past year, including a recent engagement of the national audit firm of KPMG, sponsored by the three investor groups. Indeed, all of the questions that the investors continued to raise should have been asked and answered by their consultants at KPMG, who had done extensive due diligence during the weeks they spent at Evergreen.

In typical fashion, no decision was made on an all-hands-on-deck call between the investors and Evergreen on the 21st, or after two long calls among the investors on the 22nd, even with Redmer participating in one of the calls, urging closure of the deal.

On Monday, July 24, Ren Tundermann called me, as my sons, Jack and Hank, and I were getting a new goldfish at PetSmart. The investors had decided to terminate the stock purchase agreement, claiming a material adverse condition had occurred. Without a trace of irony, they claimed that our finances were too fragile to go ahead with the agreement—a financial condition we were in largely because they had delayed the closure of the deal for more than six months. As the boys argued over which pattern of fish to get, I stared at the tanks lining the wall—thinking back to the exciting moments when Dawn, Liddy, Josh, and I had founded Evergreen, with great optimism and high hopes for implementing a better form of healthcare for our clients. Then, back in the moment, I actually felt a little relief—the long, stressful, nightmarish efforts to save the company over the past year were finally over— and we wouldn't have to fight any more.

The decision made by the investors would leave Evergreen to expire as a company, resulting in the loss of more than 100 jobs and an innovative and important option for Maryland's consumers. The value of our combined insurance and care model was captured well in this letter Liz Burger, formerly the executive director of Evergreen's PCOs, received from an Evergreen insurance client who had obtained care through one of our PCOs, after hearing of Evergreen's demise:

> When I first came to Evergreen Health Care, I was a medical mess inside and out. I had uncontrolled diabetes, boils, yeast infections, chronic depression, and chronic stomach/back pain . . . I had such bad experiences with medical providers . . . one doctor I had was taking advantage of my insurance company . . . No one ever explained anything to me. As a result . . . , I was experiencing medical burnout . . . When you get that overwhelmed, you just drop everything. I wasn't doing my morning finger stick readings, and I was not taking my diabetes medication. I didn't even want to know my numbers. At Evergreen, first I met Sara (behavioral health specialist). I had never been to a counselor before. Boy did that young lady get into my head. Together, we outlined my feelings, untwisted lots of emotions and replaced them with something positive. Most importantly, she gave me structure. Then I met Caitlin (nurse practitioner). She is the sweetest caring person. When I first started here, my A1C was 12.4. Caitlin gave me goals for my daily numbers. She gave me manageable steps. She wrote everything down, and she explained to me what the numbers mean. Now, I really understand what diabetes is, what the different insulins are, what makes them different, and how my medication and my behaviors (relat[ing] to sleep, exercise, and diet) interact. My goal is to be under 7, and I am already at 8 in only 9 months. Thanks to these ladies, I no longer have boils. My ulcer is gone. My mind is right. I feel good mentally. I understand my condition and [what it takes to manage it]. Now, I am healthy and happy. I am living a productive life . . . That is the outcome of Evergreen. I get emotional when I think about how much these ladies have done for me. When the office made the decision to close, I was worried about giving up and going back to my old place. Then I talked with Sara, and she made me realize that I can maintain this. Let me tell you, I am a different person from the day I walked into this office for the first time.

As the investors retreated, at 4 p.m. on Monday, July 31, 2017, Wayne Johnson, of Risk and Regulatory Consulting, LLC, a national receivership firm, arrived at the front door of Evergreen's headquarters. He had been appointed the receiver for Evergreen and, with his six colleagues in tow, would be responsible for liquidating the company. This entailed laying off much of the staff to save money to insure that the medical claims of Evergreen's enrollees could be paid through the rest of the year. All of the members would have their health coverage transferred to another insurer, and Evergreen would cease to exist.

A smooth-talking Floridian, Johnson plied me for information on Evergreen when we met the following morning. After getting what he needed, he politely told me it was time for me to "check out." Expecting to be terminated early in the receivership, this wasn't a great surprise. What took me aback was that he told me he wouldn't even give me a single day's notice.

So, with no further ado, I walked out of Evergreen, disillusioned, in search of a new challenge.

Conclusion

A Dozen Lessons Learned

There are many lessons to be learned from the Evergreen Health experience. Here, I describe some of them, laid out roughly in the order of where they should be considered in the chronology of starting a new program, initiative, or business. By applying these lessons from the Evergreen experience, future visionaries will be more likely to successfully implement programs and businesses that provide innovative, beneficial services to clients and society alike.

Twelve Lessons Learned

1. *Before trying to launch a new entity in response to a new government program, ascertain the level of support for the new program from the sponsoring agency.*

In order to maximize the likelihood of success, you must determine whether the funding for the operation is sufficient, whether the sponsoring agency will provide technical support, and whether there is flexibility in the rules governing the program to ensure that change can occur quickly if real-world experiences so dictate. Equally important is to identify whether the sponsoring agency is willing to provide political cover in the early years of implementation when positive results may take a few years to occur.

To illustrate this point, let me compare the implementation of our needle exchange program in Baltimore with the implementation of the CO-OP program.

The needle exchange program came with guaranteed funding from the mayor of Baltimore. It had tremendous political support from the top leaders of the city to the grassroots. We had the flexibility to set up the program as we, and the communities we served, desired (that is, using a mobile van rather than a fixed site). And, we had legal protection for the program participants with the support of the police command staff.

In contrast, with the CO-OP program, inadequate resources were provided by the sponsoring agencies of HHS and CMS (including virtually no new capital for growth). Additionally, it became clear quickly that not only was there going to be virtually no political support from CMS/HHS, they would actively "throw the CO-OPs under the bus." From the beginning of the program, CMS imposed numerous arbitrary restrictions, and the rules and formula for risk adjustment had such a negative impact on the CO-OP program that it was largely responsible for the failure of virtually every CO-OP within two years of the CO-OPs serving their first enrollees.

2. *Beware programs that result from extensive compromise.*

Programs arising from compromise legislation tend not to have strong political support, because the proponents of MORE want MORE, and opponents don't support it in the first place. This is even more likely to be true if the primary legislative/executive champion retires before implementation, leaving no one heavily invested in assuring success of that initiative.

3. *Pay attention to which major interest groups have been involved in backroom legislative negotiations on an initiative.*

If an interest group is trying to protect its market share, they are sure to try to inject language in the legislation that might tie new entrants' hands behind their backs. As an example, virtually every major interest group took part in the "sausage-making" that resulted in the Affordable Care Act. In particular, the insurance lobby pushed for rules that significantly crippled the chances of survival of new small insurers, including the CO-OPs (for example, changing grants to the new CO-OPs to loans; imposing severe restrictions on raising additional capital, precluding growth; and implementing a ban on federal funding for marketing).

These major entities generally contribute significant amounts of campaign funds to legislators, which leads to these major actors having immense political power, because most legislators are reluctant to challenge the source of all-important campaign contributions. In the case of the ACA, one of the biggest participants in the deliberations was the Blue Cross / Blue Shield Association. Thus, it was no surprise that the Blues were the big beneficiaries of the marketplace rules and the risk adjustment formula.

4. *Once it has been determined that a new program is adequately supported by the sponsoring agency, be sure that the rules and regulations that will be in place allow for at least a somewhat level playing field.*

Preferably, rules and regulations should be phased in over time to be sure that they are accomplishing their intended goals.

An example of a sensible phase-in of new rules is the Medicare Advantage Program's risk adjustment formula. With this usage of risk adjustment (a somewhat similar though not exact version of the ACA risk adjustment formula), for the first couple of years, the results of the formula were just data to ascertain if the purposes of the formula had been met. In other words, no money changed hands during this trial period. Once informed by this data, CMS made necessary changes, and eventually implemented the actual formula with little controversy. They continued to amend the risk adjustment rules many more times over the ensuing decade and a half, as experience dictated.

Compare this sensible phased-in implementation of risk adjustment in Medicare Advantage with the immediate imposition of the untried ACA risk adjustment formula and the damage it caused to most new insurers in the marketplace. I am convinced that if it, too, had been phased in over a few years and appropriate changes been made, most small insurers/CO-OPs would likely have adjusted, the market would have stabilized, and small insurers/CO-OPs would have survived.

5. *Don't do too much at once (that is, don't bite off more than you can chew).*

Both the implementation of the Evergreen CO-OP/PCO system and that of the ACA itself exemplify the problems that arise if this tenet is not followed.

Regarding the Evergreen CO-OP, several of our staff questioned whether we should have concentrated on perfecting the CO-OP before starting the PCOs—that it was too difficult to launch two startups at the same time. I concede the point, but, in my defense, the PCOs were needed to differentiate us from the rest of the market—and if we'd waited, our local foundations would likely not have funded the PCOs at all.

The Obama administration also was too quick to implement massive changes to the American health system, leading to very damaging results. For example, the federal and most state exchanges crashed at the opening of ACA enrollment. It would have been much smoother for citizens, the government, and the healthcare system alike if major aspects of the ACA had been phased in more slowly. But there is a caveat: in defense of the Obama administration, by the time of the formal implementation of the ACA (January 2014), the entire Congress was controlled by Republicans. This precluded legislative changes to fix problems that arose, because Republicans were sure to pass damaging amendments to the ACA if the act were reopened.

6. *Initially, lack of industry knowledge and/or time constraints often require new entities to rely on outside experts/vendors.*

Proceed carefully when you choose outside experts/vendors, who have you at their mercy in several ways. You often have to take their statements as the truth because of your lack of expertise. Your needed services are generally provided on their timetable, and you have little leverage even if you negotiate service levels—because you're out of business if they drop out. Going outside is also usually more expensive than taking on these duties in-house. The bottom line is that thorough vetting is necessary, lest you end up with a debacle like Care Solutions not being able to upload simple data to the CMS Edge Server.

7. *Before launching a startup in any industry, know the field!*

Take the time to talk to experts in the specific field you are trying to enter, before you launch. Even better, try to find others who began startups in your arena. They will be particularly well suited to tell you what you need to know that you did not know previously. They can point out pitfalls and likely obstacles, allowing you to address them proactively rather than reactively. For example, if we had talked to executives from other small insurance startups prior to launching Evergreen, we might have expected that CareFirst would purposely underprice us on the individual market in an effort to quickly knock us out of business. This knowledge could have led to our preemptively offering lower individual premiums ourselves to gain market share (and adjust later), rather than find ourselves with virtually no enrollees on the individual market the first year and having to react by racing to get on the group market midway through the year.

8. *Be cognizant of your naïveté.*

In the case of Evergreen, our lack of knowledge of basic health insurance practices negatively affected our initial year of operation. Even more damaging, our lack of understanding of a major component of the CO-OP program ended up contributing to our demise. Had we understood the consequences of the risk adjustment process a few months sooner, we would have tried to increase our risk adjustment score more quickly. Unfortunately, our naïveté effectively kept our eyes from seeing this obstacle to success, which precluded our dealing with it in a more timely manner.

9. *Despite the tendency to see others in public service as being on the side of the good, maintain a skeptical mindset, which allows you to see reality and fight back if necessary.*

10. *Beware entering into a regulated market with an untested regulatory formula (for example, risk adjustment).*

Enough said.

11. *If caught in a situation where the rules continue to be changed in the middle of the game, think creatively and outside the box.*

When CMS continued to change the rules on us throughout the fall of 2016, each time threatening our survival, we had to formulate whatever palatable alternative we could devise in order to survive. By thinking creatively, we actually came up with what potentially could have been a better model for long-term viability (selling the CO-OP and the PCOs to investors) than our original CO-OP proposal.

12. *Don't trust, but verify.*

When an agency imposes requirements that may mortally wound your organization, dig in and research the authority for such a requirement—as we found, when we personally went to the law books to prove CMS and Treasury were wrong about the 30% interest penalty they were about to impose on us.

Epilogue

On February 28, 2018, months after the once-profitable Evergreen Health CO-OP went into receivership, a federal judge in the United States District Court for the District of New Mexico announced a preliminary decision on a matter before him. It was a case brought by the New Mexico CO-OP, patterned after Evergreen's suit against CMS over the severely biased risk adjustment formula. Although some of the New Mexico CO-OP's claims were denied, the court ruled that the formulation of the risk adjustment formula by CMS was indeed arbitrary and capricious, and required CMS to rework the risk adjustment formula to make it more equitable.

There is absolutely no question in my mind that had we gotten such a ruling from Judge Russell in our Federal District Court case, the risk adjustment formula changes would have resulted in Evergreen's survival. Instead, we have to be satisfied with holding our heads high, knowing that the claim we pursued throughout the halls of power—to the executive branch, the legislative branch, and the judiciary—was legitimate and our efforts were worthy.

Acknowledgments

Throughout this book, I have used excerpts from several types of primary sources. Most frequently I have included portions of emails between myself and either Maryland insurance commissioner Al Redmer or senior staff at the Centers for Medicare and Medicaid Services (CMS). In all those instances I have clearly identified the sources and the fact that this was an email. Similarly, I have included portions of conversations between myself and others—at Evergreen, CMS, and with others involved in the Evergreen experience. Again, in each instance I have identified the participants and made clear that these were actual conversations that took place during the course of the story. Finally, I have used excerpts of written pieces, including letters and media articles, all of which are disclosed as such a communication.

A few specific communications merit additional referencing. In chapter 1, Dr. Berwick's Triple Aim was first referenced in an article in the journal *Health Affairs*, May/June 2008; the information from Ken Lalime was communicated in a phone call on February 10, 2018. In chapter 6, the quote I gave Paul Demko was reported in *Politico* by Dan Diamond on May 27, 2016—"Ohio co-op dies, resurrecting questions about program." The *Baltimore Sun* editorial in chapter 7, "Can Evergreen force Obamacare to live up to its promise?," appeared on June 13, 2016. The first CMS letter in chapter 9 is dated September 9, 2016; see https://www.cms.gov/CCIIO/Programs-and-Initiatives/Premium-Stabiliza tion-Programs/Downloads/Risk-Corridors-for-2015-FINAL.PDF. The letter from Congressman Fred Upton to HHS Secretary Sylvia Burwell in chapter 9 is dated September 20, 2016; see https://archives-energycommerce.house.gov /sites/republicans.energycommerce.house.gov/files/documents/114/letters /20160920HHS.pdf.

Index